Incense has fascinated m
part of many ceremonies
to making and using your own incense, giving details of its
historical background and providing practical formulas for
personal and group rituals.

INCENSE

Its Ritual Significance, Preparation and Use

by

Leo Vinci

Illustrations by Roger L. Fitzpatrick

THE AQUARIAN PRESS LIMITED
Wellingborough, Northamptonshire

First published 1980

ISBN 0 85030 211 0 (UK)
ISBN 0 87728 464 4 (USA)

Photoset by
Specialised Offset Services Limited, Liverpool
and printed in Great Britain by
Weatherby Woolnough Ltd,
Wellingborough, Northants.

CONTENTS

ACKNOWLEDGEMENTS

I would like to give my special thanks to Martin Vincent who undertook the task of reading the original manuscript. I also give my thanks to Andy Bull who supplies me with most of the ingredients for my personal use and with whom I have had many useful discussions.

I would like to dedicate this book to Shek Chang Wong, who has the quiet wisdom of his ancestors.

INTRODUCTION

The barge she sat in, like a burnished throne,
Burn'd on the water; the poop was beaten gold,
Purple the sails, and so perfumed, that
The winds were love-sick with them.

William Shakespeare, *Anthony and Cleopatra*

What can the reader expect from this book? Primarily, the knowledge of making and using incense! Nothing has captivated mankind more than this fascinating and bewitching practice, even if only pursued for 'just making nice smells'. We find its use in the ceremonies and rites of the Christians, Pagans, Hindus, Buddhists, and others, for they have all delighted in its odoriferous perfumes and smokes, and time may have even strengthened its enchanting allure.

Many things have been used in the composition of incense: gums, resins, woods and barks, oils, and even hallucinatory drugs, of which more later. First we will take a brief look at its use down the centuries and some of the ways in which earlier civilizations have regarded and used it. (In picking through the bones of history I have tried not to raise too dry a dust.) Next we touch upon perfumes, flower oils, and anointing oils (as many of the ingredients used are common to these as well as incenses), with a brief explanation of their use. You will find incense formulas or recipes for your own personal or group use. These have been gathered from many sources and I have been using most of them for a long time now. Some are from ancient records and manuscripts and have thus become 'tradition'; some are from friends who have been persuaded to part with them; others have been created to meet the needs of personal or group use. They will form an excellent basis for your immediate needs and will supply you with an adequate stock cupboard for the temple or home. They can also be used as a beginning for any future work should you wish to experiment later. Finally, you will find a table of planetary hours with simple instructions for choosing the correct times for making your incenses, if you decide to make them for yourself, as I sincerely hope you will. This table can also be used for many other ritual and occult matters, as suggested, so do *not* restrict its use to this work only.

Importance of Incense

Incense is of vital importance in ritual, and should, therefore, be used correctly. The use of the incense appropriate to the operation is an important adjunct to success in ritual work. If you are ever in doubt as to which incense to use, do not let this worry you too much in the beginning, since most have this problem initially. Simply use one of the general or all-purpose incenses rather than a possibly incorrect one, which may lessen your chances of success. It is an excellent practice to always have an ample supply of good, all-round incense, in case of doubt, or if the incense you need at a critical point of the proceedings runs out. Regard your general incense as 'first-aid' when you need it. However, you must make every effort to see that you use the correct incense for your operation, and learn the correct correspondences, for you cannot make an 'atmosphere of earth' for an operation which is for a 'creature of water'.

Correspondences

Man, to all intents and purposes, 'swims in' and breathes an 'atmosphere' of air. In much the same way a fish swims in and breathes an 'atmosphere' of water, extracting oxygen from the water by use of its gills, as Man extracts oxygen from the air by use of his lungs. Yet, you cannot catch a fish, throw it on the lawn, and expect it to live just because it breathes oxygen. You have to provide your fish with an area or space in which to live, such as a tank, bowl, or a pond dug out for them in the garden, lined with a suitable material to prevent their 'atmosphere' escaping. When you have done this, you fill the given area with water, and finally put in the fish, having created a suitable environment for them to live in. Putting plants in the water completes the oxygen cycle, as plants and trees do for mankind.

Likewise, if Man wants to survive in an atmosphere or

space other than his own, such as water, he must take his 'atmosphere' with him. He can use a diving machine or suit which encloses him, or cylinders that feed air directly into his lungs. Then he can use the element of water, which is not his true one, or go into spaces or areas that lack sufficient air for his needs or where the air is unsuitable for his use.

Correct Preparation

The ritualist is in a similar position, in that *he* must prepare the area or space and provide a suitable atmosphere. It is not done *for* him. First you define the area or space to be occupied or worked in. This is usually your temple, magic circle, or the room you are using. If working outside you can define your area with, say, four large stones, perhaps of distinctive shape, at the four cardinal points of the compass. They do not need to be special. Having defined your area, you then create the 'atmosphere' by the appropriate ritual and/or incense(s). Burning the appropriate incense, among other things, is a form of protocol which is given according to rank or station. Thus, the higher the rank, the greater the protocol required. This is also why I said at the outset that you cannot prepare your area or space for one element if you are working by invocation for another.

Incense is a very subtle substance which vibrates on many planes of existence by the use of appropriate ingredients. The fine particles of incense smoke in the air can act as a point of contact, or 'support', for the finer elements which vibrate at a higher rate. The prime thing to remember is that it is *we* who do the preparation.

There is often great disappointment in store for the beginner who assumes that just because he has burnt some incense, censed everything in sight, and recited a few conjurations, a spirit or power will appear. If you decide to try to contact a spirit or power, you must first create an atmosphere and area which is agreeable to it. You would not enter or stay in a room that was unpleasant or in which you could not breath – why should they?

Incense, then, plays a very important part in the performance of rituals. The incense 'problem' in Christian worship was a highly emotive and controversial issue in the latter half of the nineteenth century. We may regard the matter as somewhat ridiculous and a 'storm-in-a-teacup' affair today, but great passions were roused, and still can be. As other writers have rightly observed, incense is a unique and strange phenomenon, for it assails you not only on a physical level, but also on a psychological one, and may even be somewhat addictive in habit according to personal temperament.

Yet, a candle-lit church or temple, a combination of choir and organ in solemn music, ritual and regalia, stained-glass windows, thurible wafting the sweet smoke of incense – all exercise an atavistic and inexplicable power.

A Cautionary Note

The old magicians were most particular to have the appropriate incense, or 'suffumigations' when they were working for any specific purpose. They always took great care to see that the correct ingredients, appropriate to the planet or constellation under which they were working, were used, or combined. It was their belief that the correct odours had the power to attract the planetary spirits, or powers.

Early writings always credited certain perfumes with the 'power to gather together', while others had the power 'to drive away'. Many incenses are said to be 'active' and thus are 'commanding', and these were used by many magicians and occultists who worked under 'Will'. Some incenses are of the 'passive' type (the incense sticks of Indian origin are mainly of this classification), and this type has the effect of making a person 'open', and hence a channel for the forces to use. As far as invoking 'good' forces is concerned, it is the *channel* which must be (relatively) uncontaminated, else the force will not manifest in its purest form. Hence the danger of invoking a Mars force by a person with, say, an inordinately bad temper, for such a person would be more likely to respond to the negative, destructive side of the force, rather than to the constructive or positive. This is why many teachers, schools and groups subscribe to the traditional view that rigorous character training should ideally preceed any major occult work. Further, who but an idiot or practitioner of the Left Hand Path would wish to serve as a channel for forces whose very nature is 'contaminating'?

Hallucinatory Additives

It is for this reason that I am unhappy about any additive to incenses that may be the cause of hallucinations, disorientation, etc. While some may consider it fun to try, it is to be rejected by all but the most experienced occultist. The inclusion of ingredients of a narcotic or illusory nature may give more than you bargained for, especially if these are added to an incense used in group working. This practice, especially if done without the knowledge and consent of others (a practice definitely to be frowned upon), may quite often show up a weak link in the chain of the group, perhaps one you did not even know existed.

Books written on the subject of the 'Black Arts', and other sensationalist works, often advocate the use of narcotic or hallucinatory ingredients, but their suggested formulas invariably fail to invoke the force or spirit expected by the aspirant, and succeeds instead, if it can be called success, in merely attracting those unevolved, and, usually, unhygienic spirits, or Elementals, which delight and thrive in the atmosphere created by the drug-inspired confusion of the well-meaning, but inept amateur. Though they exist and are used, it is for this reason that certain types of incense (e.g. necromantic) have been omitted from this book.

The use of narcotic or hallucinogenic additives tend to be addictive. A small amount added at the beginning will slowly increase as tolerance increases; thus, dependency on the additive will likewise be increased, but not any acquired ability as a result of its use. It has to be admitted that history has numerous recorded examples of the use of narcotic additives with seemingly excellent results (the most obvious being the Delphic Oracle). But it has to be remembered that the people who were subjected to these intoxicating effects were highly trained in these matters and under the guidance of temples and arcane schools, and, further, that they were chosen because of their suitability for this particular facet of the occult arts.

Gaining your occult ability the hard way may be slow and very frustrating, but it is lasting; the only way in the end is to 'hew it out' for yourself.

Anything which may endanger the health of the magician/occultist should be eschewed, especially as regards 'health' on levels other than the physical. There is little point in trying to keep the physical vehicle in the best shape we can, if the 'driver' is 'drunk'. Disorder, or at the worst, disaster may prove to be the likely results of such practices.

CHAPTER ONE

THE HISTORICAL BACKGROUND

Egyptian

The Egyptians were great practitioners in the manufacture and use of incense, and they brought the compounding of their incenses to a very high art. Many of their ideas regarding incense share a common basis with those of other peoples and their beliefs, as will be seen. Perhaps the most famous of all the Egyptian incenses is *Kyphi* (sometimes *Khyphi*). This is a most elaborate compound of ingredients, and its manufacture was itself a very special temple rite, and a most secret one. It is said to be most beneficial in its effects, and this is explained by Plutarch in the following manner: 'The incense has sixteen ingredients, which is a square out of a square, the ingredients being things that delight in the night. It has the power to lull people to sleep, brighten the dreams, and loosen the tensions of daily anxiety, by bringing calm and quiet to all who breathed it.' The ingredients were mixed to a secret ritual, to the accompaniment of chanting of sacred texts. It had the mysterious significance of harmony and order.

Frankincense

One of the ingredients of *Kyphi* is the ever popular frankincense. As with all other nations of the world up to the present day, the Egyptians valued frankincense very highly. To obtain this very valuable commodity they organized expeditions to the Land of Punt, as this was the area where the frankincense was chiefly gathered. It is a gum resin of the trees of the Boswellia family (*Boswellia Thurifera*). The Land of Punt was on the hinterland of the Somali coast of East Africa. Pliny refers to frankincense as one of the products of Arabia (Hadramant), saying that the Sabaei alone behold the tree which produces frankincense, and of these only 3000 families, by virtue of hereditary succession. The trees were considered sacred, and while pruning them or gathering the resin the men must be free from pollution by sexual intercourse, or contact with the dead.

Herodotus waxes more lyrical, and claims that winged serpents guard the trees, and have been driven off by the burning of styrax (storax.) When harvested it was carried to Sabota, where the priests claimed a tithe of the frankincense in honour of their god Sabis, and until this was paid, none of it could be disposed of. As frankincense was the gum of what was regarded as a holy species of tree and the gum was collected with religious precautions, perhaps it was thought to possess an intrinsic virtue, like the gum of the Samora tree – the idea being that it was the 'blood' of an animate and divine plant. Plutarch gives a list of sixteen ingredients that were used in the preparation of this most sacred of the Egyptian incenses: honey, wine, raisins, sweet rush, resin, myrrh, frankincense, seselis, calamus, asphalt, thryon, dock, both kinds of arcouthelds, caramum and orris root. It has to be admitted, however, that a great many formulas for *Kyphi* exist. Sir Wallace Budge, for example, gives tchet oil as one of the ingredients.

Odour of the Gods

The Egyptian gods, in keeping with other beliefs right up to the present day, were said to have a wonderful odour. Today we call this the 'odour of sanctity', some even claiming that many good people who have been canonized have displayed this sweet odour in death. To those whom he loves, Osiris transfers his odour, as did Isis, and especially to the dead. At the anointing of the corpse, the 'perfume on the head of Horus' was especially sought after for placing on the head of the deceased. In Egypt the burning of the various kinds of incense was an important part of any rite, as each ingredient had its own magical and mystical properties. In their worship of the Sun God Ra, the Egyptians burnt incense to him three times during the course of the day. The first was as he rose in the morning, personified by the Sun, when he was greeted with the burning of resin. The second time was when he stood at his zenith at noon, when he was offered myrrh; and lastly as he sank in the West in the evening, when he was given the final offering of *Kyphi*.

Hindu

The Hindus have always been fond of pleasant odours, and India was already celebrated for its perfumes in ancient times. Incense from Arabia was a very early import, but many native kinds of sweet smelling materials have long been in use – benzoin and other gum resins, seeds, roots, dried flowers, and fragrant woods. These materials are burned ritually in public, or privately in domestic usage. Perhaps one of the most popular items is sandalwood, used both in ancient times in the temple or the home, and in modern times as an ingredient in the incense sticks which they export in vast quantities. The Indian *Dainyal* or sybil in the Hindu Kush attempts to gain temporary inspiration with the aid of sacred plants or trees. She places a cloth over her head and inhales the smoke from a fire that has been made with the twigs of the sacred cedar. She is seized with convulsions, falls to the ground senseless and, in this state she gives her prophecy.

In modern Hinduism the use of incense is fairly widespread. In the cult of Siva, it is burnt daily by the priest before the stone representing the god at Orissa, and perfumes are also placed upon it. Camphor and incense are burned before the image of Krishna.

Jewish

The frequent references to incense in the Old Testament have given rise to the view that its use goes back to very early times among the Jews. In fact, the Authorized Version often used the word to refer to the aroma of the burnt offerings, and the ancient Hebrews may have regarded the use of incense, so popular with the Babylonians, as the mere trappings of idolatry. It was regarded at first in much the same way by the early Christian church, which associated its use with paganism. In fact, this misconception arises from the rendering of the word *k(e)toreth* as incense when, strictly speaking, it means the savoury smoke of burnt offerings. The word frankincense is *l(e)bonah*, (in Arabic, *luban*), meaning 'sweet resinous gum'. These two Hebrew words at first were quite distinct in meaning, though latterly the first became synonymous with the second; thus, *k(e)toreh* also came to mean incense.

Scholars now generally agree, that the burning of incense was not introduced into the Judaic ritual until about the seventh century B.C. Once it was adopted, however, it became more and more important in acts of worship. This first incense used was compounded of few ingredients – stacte, onycha, galbanum and pure frankincense – and its mixing by the priests was regarded with much the same reverence accorded to the manufacture of *Kyphi* by the Egyptians. It was burned with the meat offerings and with the first fruits, and on its own, at morning and evening on a special altar, The Altar of Incense, or in censers. It was taken, once a year on the Day of Atonement, inside the Inner Sanctum of the Temple.

Ezekiel 'one whom God strengthens' makes no reference to incense in his description of the reformed ritual (Ezekiel, 40). The first distinct reference to its use in the cult of Jahweh is in Jeremiah, 6:20: 'To what purpose cometh there to me incense from Sheba, and the sweet cane [calmus] from a far country?' Some references in the Biblical account show that incense is not required. Once it had been admitted, however, it came to be a regular part of the ritual, and is very frequently cited in the priestly code. Incense was offered either, by itself, or, as a part of other sacrifices. It was burned in censers, as on the Day of Atonement, when the high priest appeared before the mercy seat (Leviticus, 16:12), or when Aaron passed through the congregation to stay the plague with his censer and incense, an act of atonement and fumigation (Numbers, 16:46).

Greek

It seems that incense, in the sense of gums and resins as we know them, were not used by the Greeks until after the Homeric period. Pliny says that people knew only 'the smell of cedar wood and citrus as it rose in volumes of smoke from the sacrifice.' The wood of odoriferous trees, of cedar and myrtle, was burned in houses for its fragrant smell. In common with others, the Greeks considered a sweet and fragrant odour was pleasant to the gods, thus making sacrifice and prayer more acceptable to them. Before the eighth century B.C., incense as such, was not used. Schrader is of the opinion that it may have been introduced through the cult of Aphrodite, and it is certainly traditionally held to have come from Phoenicia through Cyprus, where it was used in her cult. It was imported into Greece as a commercial venture from Arabia at a later date. The word 'frankincense' was a foreign derivation. In accordance with the customs of other nations it was burned with bloody sacrifices, both as an offering to the gods, and a fumigation for the evil odours produced.

It was offered with fruit, cakes, wheat and so on, or on its own as a separate offering both in the cult of the gods, or in domestic ritual. In the cults of the gods it was burnt to Zeus Meiluchios, to Hermes, Sosipolis, and to Demeter before consulting the Oracle at Patrae. Incense was quite often presented as a gift, from one person to another. Large amounts were used, as the inventory lists of some temples show. In the rites of certain divinities it was offered with cakes of honey, quite often without being burned. The incense was sometimes thrown on the altar so as to mingle with the smoke of the sacrifice; the sacrifice itself was often filled with incense before burning, or it was simply thrown into braziers that were standing on, or near, the altar; it was even burnt outside the temple itself. It was, naturally, burnt in vessels that could be held in the hand. In the Orphic cult, incenses of many different kinds were used, as the hymns show.

Buddhism

As with many religions in their initial stage, incense was unknown to early Buddhism, opposed as it was to external ritualism. In the course of time, however, they also succumbed to its use, especially Northern Buddhism, where it became very general. In Ceylon, perfumes and flowers are offered before the image of the Buddah, though it is in the Tibet of old that the use of incense is most prevalent, for here it is used in the initiation ceremony of monks and is part of the daily ritual of monasteries and the village priesthood. It is offered to gain support of the good spirits and it is very prominent at festivals in which 'clouds of incense fill the air', also at baptisms, exorcisms, and many other ceremonies. Incense and perfumes form one of the five sensuous offerings, which are one of the seven stages of worship. These seven offerings are essential, and in them flowers and incense occur as early as the seventh century.

In the Japanese branch of Buddhism, incense is in common use, and has influenced the native religion of Shinto.

The Chinese seem to have always employed incense, public and private usage being widespread. Incense is offered in temples as a part of the daily worship and ritual, is burnt at festivals and processions, and is offered to the household deities and before ancestral tablets. Its use is deemed desirable when consulting the gods, the I Ching, or any magical ceremonies. The burning of incense also plays an important part in Chinese funeral ceremonies and processions, it acts both as a fumigant and an offering to the deceased, where it gratifies the olfactory nerves of the departing soul. In Canton, on the third week of the twelfth month, all the dirt is swept out of the house, and three sticks of incense are used to drive out the demon of poverty.

Roman

In the religion of Rome, one of the most important of what is known as the *libamina*, or bloodless offerings, was *tus*, meaning both incense and frankincense, and no ritual could be said to be complete without it. It has been strongly suggested that this consisted initially of odoriferous woods and herbs, as described by Ovid, in his account of the Palilia, the Shepherd's Festival, such as olive, laurel branches, pitchwood and Sabine herbs. Later the gums and resins came to be used instead of, or in addition to, the above – frankincense (*masculum tus*), myrrh, costum, crocus, and so on. Incense was offered by itself, in public or in private, and was also offered to the *lares familiares*, or household gods. It was naturally much in evidence at magical ceremonies. The manner in which it was used was either to burn it on the greater altars, in braziers, or on small portable altars called *foci turibulum*. The incense was carried in a casket called an *acerra*, which was used in funerary ceremonies, from which it was taken to be burned.

In the blood sacrifices, they began by burning incense, saffron and laurel. As the animal for sacrifice was led up to the altar, the altar itself was sprinkled with incense and wine. Finally it was offered with the blood of the sacrifice, and burned with the *exta*, the chief internal organs. It was used during the persecutions under the Roman Emperor Decius c.200-251, who most ruthlessly persecuted the Christians for their faith. It also became symbolic of the Christians who renounced their faith, which they proved by burning a few grains of incense on an altar before an image, or to the Emperor. Christians who renounced their faith in this manner were known as *Thurificati*. This was a symbolic act of apostasy, for it tested the individual's loyalty to the State, and loyalty to the State meant loyalty to the State religion.

Christianity

Christianity was slow to adopt incense into its rites. The services of the early church were very simple and incense (save as a purification) was shunned as something Jewish or pagan. Some, however, argue that the Jewish connection should have made it more acceptable. *Pererinatio ad Loca Santa*, published by Gamurrini in 1887, contains the account of travels by a lady, ascribed by general consent to a certain Silvia of Aquitain, during the years 385-388. They give a full and graphic description to the services at which the pilgrim was present during her visit to Jerusalem, which included Holy Week. The *original* spelling of the manuscript is preserved: 'Dictus ergo his tribus psalmis, et factis orationibus tribus, ecce etiam thimiatasia inferuntur intra spelunca Anastasis ut tota basilica Anastasis repleatur ordoribus.' (Censers were taken in the cave [of the Holy Sepulchre] 'so that the whole church [which the Greeks call Anastasis, and which we call the Church of the Holy Sepulchre] was filled with the odour.') The use of incense here is unmistakably ceremonial. In the years 385-388 its ceremonial usage was evidently not a novel one, but already well established. It would be no straining of probability to suppose that it dated back to the founding of the church by Constantine. The *Liber Pontificalis* contains, under the pontificate of Silvester (314-355), inventories of the furniture of the churches built by Constantine at Rome, and several of these include golden censers.

Many church authorities have alleged that the reason for the omission of incense is that it was not in use in the church for at least 300 years from Apostolic times. In view of the evidence above, especially for Jerusalem, it would be fair to conclude that censers in these churches were intended to be used ceremonially. I am sure that even these early dates do not mark the beginning of its use and that it was obviously well established by then. After the fifth century incense was slowly but increasingly used in the church. By the fourteenth century, it had become part of the established ritual of High Mass and other services, such as Vespers, the consecration of churches and processions, and funerals.

Although incense was used in Jewish ceremonial, and while such a prophecy as 'From the rising of the sun even unto the going down of the same my name shall be great among the Gentiles; and in every place incense shall be offered unto my name' (Malachi, 1:11) may seem to point to its continued use in the new dispensation; though it was one of the offerings of the Magi, (frankincense and myrrh) at Bethlehem, and though its use is referred to in the Apocalypse, there is no evidence that it was part of early church ritual according to some writers; indeed various writers employed strong words against its use. Though some of the Fathers spoke of it as a type of prayer, many of them did not. Tertulian says, 'not one penneyworth of incense do I offer Him.' Athenagoras declared that 'God does not require sweet smell of flowers or incense.' Arnobius, referring to the fact that the early Romans did not use it, maintains that Christians may safely neglect its use. Lactantius tells us that odours are not desired by God and agrees with the Neo-Platonist writers, that frankincense and the like should not be offered to him.

The fact, as with many other things, that its usage was Jewish may have tended to make the early Christians neglect it, but its pagan associations and the common practice that Christians should offer a few grains of incense to the gods or upon the altar of the Emperor, as a sign of the renunciation of their faith, probably proved a stronger deterrent. Incense was, however, used for fumigation as a sanitary precaution, at burials for example, or in places with a disagreeable odour. The Apostolic Canons refer to the use of incense at the Eucharist, but this is probably a later interpolation. It was used at the vigil offices on Sunday towards the end of the fourth century.

Islam

In the Islamic religion proper, incense is not to be found, but it is common to find it offered at the shrines of saints, and it is permitted, by tradition, as perfume for a deceased person. Muslims in India, possibly under the influence of Hinduism, use it in their rites (circumcision, marriage, funerals), as it is supposed to have the ability to keep evil spirits at bay. Among the Muslims it is burned in houses on braziers, and at marriage ceremonies, when it is burnt in a *mibkharah*.

In keeping with other cults it is a common adjunct to magical ceremonies, to counteract the evil eye, for example, or for use in the 'science' of *da'wah*, a method of incantation. The letters of the name of the person for whom the incantation is being made indicate the required perfume. The materials used for incenses are: frankincense, benzoin, storax, coriander seed and aloes among others.

CHAPTER TWO

FLOWERS AND PERFUMES

This is not the first work by any means to propose to the reader the possibility of using and counteracting the action of one perfume against another. This was suggested as far back as 1937 by Carolyn H. Hayes, and perhaps even earlier by others. A large amount of the material presented here is a synthesis of traditional material and theory gathered over a long period and taken from a wide variety of sources. By the welding together of many isolated facts and bringing them together under one heading, it is hoped that those who are prepared to give time to the subject will find it a very fruitful line of research.

A person lacking an extrovert nature and who tends to shyness may try counteracting this by the use of Ambergris, while those who feel they may be lacking in sympathy and understanding can try using Violet (by having a small phial with cotton wool which has been soaked in a few drops of the perfume.) The lover of Ambergris who feels that he, or she, may spoil a situation or opportunity through appearing too high-spirited or reckless, may find they can balance this by using Lily of the Valley. Those who tend to be obdurate in their point of view, which may possibly lead to controversy and dispute, may find that Lavender or Violet can counterbalance these tendencies.

Flower Perfumes
The perfumes of flowers and herbs have always pleased mankind, but not all nature's creations are endowed with pleasing odours or good intent. The herbs Rue, Hellebore (both White and Black), Asaffoedita, Sulphur and Dragon's Blood are some of the 'herbs of aggression' used in witchcraft.

We use flowers on so many commemorative or important days in our lives and, naturally, we prefer those flowers that give the most pleasing scents. Births, deaths and weddings are all occasions when we give flowers and their perfumes fill the air. The bride carries flowers from the 'garden of Nature' in front of her on her wedding day, they are held over the 'garden' of her body – a fairly obvious analogy. We need not go into the once secret code of love which used the 'language of the flowers'. By use of the appropriate blossoms whole messages could be sent it seems, and ladies of propriety could, by use of a single bloom, tell an over-persistent lover a message that could never pass her lips.

In keeping with other nations we use them in our funerary arrangements. Many are of the opinion that flowers have completely replaced the incense smoke (used as well as flowers in the past) on which the spirit of the deceased was borne to the heavens. The wreaths of old were nearly always circular; now they take many other shapes or are just sprays. The circular wreath of flowers was, and still is, the most effective, because it was in effect a 'magic circle' to protect or bind the deceased spirit or soul, so preventing it from haunting the living. Now let us take a look at some of the tradition regarding perfumes and flowers.

Ambergris
This is a perfume that tends to be used by people who are bold and audacious in their actions, the extroverts of life. Everything tends to get done in the 'grand manner'.

Carnation (White)
Most claim that this is a perfume/flower used by people who are religiously inclined, and by those desirous of developing a religious spirit.

Carnation (Red)
This is held to be the perfume/flower of those who tend to make things 'larger than life', by exaggeration, intentional or otherwise, boasting, being very concerned with 'appearances', and with the kind of impression they are making on others.

Cherry Blossom
The person who likes this perfume is said to have an easy-going nature, that does not push itself forward to take the centre of the stage. By and large they prefer to wait in the wings until they are called.

Cypress, Sandalwood and Vervain
It is held that those who seek the unusual and the curious, are attracted to these scents; the out-of-the-ordinary or unconventional attracts them.

Geranium
This is for the active, the daring, those who pioneer, clear the ground and are prepared to fight for what they want, have, and can get.

Heliotrope
People who are found to be fond of this perfume are usually not afraid to be in the front line of things, liking to see and be seen! Kind and generous to a fault when allowed to 'have their head', but tending to be somewhat tyranical and authoritarian when thwarted, their sin is said to be pride.

Honeysuckle
Held to be the perfume/flower of people with an agile and versatile mind, whose thoughts are elsewhere even whilst speaking to you, or when you are speaking to them. Difficult to impress with another point of view – yours of course!

Hyacinth
Those who tend to be hasty or rash are said to be users of this perfume, perhaps even inclined to be erratic or capricious at times so that you cannot guess what they may get up to next.

Lavender and Rosemary
From those who possess calm, wisdom, and a circumpsect or provident nature, you may be able to trace the perfume or scent of Lavender. Combined with Rosemary, you have a nature that is said to be of conventional inclination, sometimes even thought to be rather sober and staid.

Lily of the Valley
Those of modest disposition may be found using this perfume, the retiring or shy, shunning the limelight, preferring and performing in the background.

Mint
A very 'active' odour, so do not try to better a lover of this

scent, especially if it is in business affairs. It shows one who
has ability and great accumen in that sphere of life. If you
can also smell the scent of Cloves – 'then depart and trust
them not'!

Magnolia and Musk
It is said that those who are obstinate and inclined to be
argumentative, liking controversy and dispute, by their
nature are drawn to these two perfumes, and, if they think
they are right, will never give an inch.

Pansy
People who favour this perfume are held to give no quarter,
and are unable to accept half-measures. They are either a
true and faithful friend, or an implacable, resolute enemy. It
is all or nothing.

Patchouli
A perfume, it is claimed, for those who have strong passions
and one which sometimes exercises an evil influence on the
moral character, if that nature is not controlled.

Red Rose
No disputing that this is the perfume/flower of those of a
passionate and loving nature. All thoughts of an amorous
nature are aroused by this perfume, and it is associated with
the tendency to be 'in love with love'.

Stephanotis
The lovers of pleasure are drawn to this perfume, arousing a
'desire to be loved and caressed'. It tends to give thoughts of
a voluptuous and sensual nature.

Verbena
The users of Verbena are said to be those who have a love of
good food, always have a well-stocked larder and wine
cellar, and simply enjoy the good things of life.

Violet
This is generally thought to soften the nature, making it
sympathetic and refined, perhaps even bordering on
timidity. It is often worn by people who respect convention,
disliking strife – hence the term 'a shrinking violet'.

Wallflower

Used by people who tend to be over-sensitive, having a great ability to see a meaning you never intended, and who are quite often found to be living very much in the past.

White Rose

The perfume of those who are lazy or indolent, disliking activity; those who 'like to stand and stare', and if they have not got the time to do this – they either take it or make it!

CHAPTER THREE

ANOINTING AND ANOINTING OILS

Many of the ingredients that are common to incenses, are also common to anointing oils and it is therefore right that these should have a place in any work on compounding incenses. They are, like incense, an important aspect of any magical ritual, though in the early stages they are not used as much as incense. That anointing oils should never be prepared from crude ingredients may seem an obvious statement, but it must be stressed that they must be prepared from the finest ingredients you can afford, otherwise all you will get is an unprepossessing sludge, which will do very little for the person on whom it is to be placed.

Anointing oils are made to smell so beautiful because they are a necessary symbolism, an adjunct to any form of 'elevation'. You would hardly feel elevated if some foul smelling oil were poured over your head. It is one of the most important of the magical/religious concepts, that virtue, holiness and divine power were impregnated in these holy anointing oils, and therefore it must follow that any person or thing anointed with this oil must likewise be endowed or impregnated with the virtue or holiness that it imparts. Anointing is not only a privilege: it is a *responsibility*, not to be taken lightly.

Anointing is a major part of any ritual, religious or royal ceremony, involving the installation, elevation or consecration of kings, queens, high-priests, a member of the church, and so forth. People so ordained were held to hold spiritual and temporal power here on earth. As the body is reputed to enclose the Divine Spark – the spirit or Soul of Man – it was consecrated to God, as any temple or church is, by Rite of Dedication, for the body is regarded as the 'Temple of the Soul'.

The Process of Anointing

The most common form of anointing was to pour oil upon
the head, then the forehead was marked with the finger (the
index finger preferably, but sometimes the little finger was
used) between the eyebrows. The Talmud tell us that 'they
anointed kings after the form of a crown, but priests after
the form of an X.' The head must always be anointed first;
if the lower centres are to be anointed, they are so in turn,
after the head.

It could be shown, or suggested, that by ending with the
anointing of the feet, this follows the course of the Sun on its
journey through the *natural* zodiac, from Aries to Pisces.
Starting with the head (ruled by Aries), then the hands
(ruled by Gemini), then the heart, the chest or breast (ruled
by Leo for the heart and Cancer for the chest and breasts).
Sometimes the generative organs (ruled by Scorpio) are
included. There is often a valid reason for this custom, but if
it is being done for cheap sensationalism it loses any validity
it may in theory have. Sometimes it is the practice to put
some of the anointing oil on the index finger of the person
being anointed, who then, *after* anointing, performs the act
in private, as they will then have the authority to do so.
Finally the feet (ruled by Pisces) are anointed.

Anointing Ritual

Here is given a small anointing ritual that you may find
useful as a basis to prepare one for your own needs. The
point in the ritual marked (+) is the suggested point of
anointing.

Forehead

'The light of the body is the eye: therefore if thy eye be
single, thy whole body shall be full of light. But if thy eye be
evil, thy whole body shall be full of darkness. If therefore the
light that is in thee be darkness, how great is that darkness!
(+) Let the Eye of Knowledge be opened so that the Light of
Knowledge and Wisdom dispels the darkness of ignorance,
that the dark corners of the mind be illumined so that
ignorance will be given no place in which to hide and
multiply. For the Light shineth in the darkness; and
darkness comprehendeth it not.'

Hands

'Let thy hands be ever open in friendship and generosity, to do good works and to aid those in need of help, the clenched fist can do naught of this. Stretch forth thy hand to heal, that signs and wonders may be done in the name of the Creator. In the mornings sow thy seed, and in the evening withold not thine hand from those who ask thy aid. (+) Whatsoever thy hands findeth to do, do it with all thy might, for there is no work, nor device, nor knowledge, nor wisdom in the grave, wither thou goest, for we fall into the hands of the Lord, and not into the hands of men; for as His Majesty is, so is His Mercy.'

Heart
'Let thy heart be blessed with love and compassion, for the Lord seeth not as man seeth; man looketh on the outward appearance, but the Lord looketh upon the heart. (+) Let the heart be opened wide with compassion, to bind up the wounds of the broken-hearted, proclaim liberty to those captive, and open the prison of the physical of them that are bound. For out of the abundance of the heart the mouth speaketh. Let not your heart be troubled. Believe ye in God? Believe then in his Son also!'

Feet
'Ponder the path at thy feet, and let all thy ways be firmly established. Turn neither to the right hand, nor to the left, and remove thy feet from evil. Then thou shalt understand righteousness, discrimination and equity; yea every good path. He brought thee out of the pit, out of the miry clay, and has set thy feet upon a rock, and will establish thy goings, for His word is a lamp unto thy feet and a light unto thy path. Can two walk together, except they be agreed? (+) May the Lord be thy mentor and companion, thou shalt need no other. May he guide thee on the path that leads from the dark Land of Ignorance into the Light.'

Blessing
Give a Blessing over the anointed person of the Balanced Cross at the points marked (+).
   'May the blessing of the Father-Mother-Creator (+), the Son (+) and the Holy Ghost, (or *Shekinah* [+]), bless you, keep you, and watch over you from this day forth and for ever more. Amen.'
   The participants in the ceremony here bow to the person who has been anointed, *after* the person who has done the

anointing. It can be done together as a group, or each person separately, which I think is preferable, but it must be remembered that you are *not* bowing to the *person*, but to the *Power* he, or she, now represents. There is no *personal* glorification in this.

The above is a general idea of how a Ritual of Anointing may be composed for group use. It has been taken deliberately from only one source, the Scriptures, simply to show that it is possible to adapt materials for personal use. It has been kept very simple in order to show that the composition of such formula should be well within the ability of everyone. You are by no means restricted to the Bible; naturally, you can use the Sacred Books of any nation or religion. You do not even have to employ religious works, for any lines which are suitable to the work in hand may be used. The main, and perhaps the *only* consideration, is that you should be moved emotionally by what is being said as well as done. Even the most tongue-tied have become eloquent under the emotional sway of a moving ritual. You can vary the form to suit your needs: it need not be as given above. You can, for example, compile a ritual which places the anointing at the end, all sections being read together instead of separately (though I prefer the former).

Before anointing, the hands should be washed well, in Hyssop preferably. You can make this up with one ounce (25g) of Hyssop to a pint (550ml) of hot water. I would let the infusion stand for at least fifteen minutes before you use it. Otherwise wash thoroughly with a high quality soap, using a little perfume or oil afterwards.

A further suggestion that could be used by a person officiating at an anointing ceremony is an adaption of Psalm 51. In fact the Psalms are a very fruitful field to work, using imagination as your 'spade'. The word 'me' is removed from the first line and the name of the person substituted. The remainder of the Psalm is modified for the occasion, according to the sex of the person being anointed, in the following manner:

'Have mercy upon 'John Smith' O God according to thy loving kindness:
According unto the multitude of thy tender mercies blot out his transgressions.
Wash him thoroughly from his iniquity,

And cleanse him from his sin, ...
... Purge him with hyssop and he shall be clean,
Wash him, and he shall be whiter than snow, etc. ...

Period of Appointment

Anointing is not something to be taken lightly. It is not simply a matter of placing a few dabs of oil here and there and leaving it at that. Prior to anointment there should have been a period of 'appointment'. This period, the length of which is defined by the rules of the teacher, group or school, can be anything from one year, to seven or even more (one year is far too short if the subject is to be taken seriously, as it should be). During the period of appointment, those who are in a position to confer authority by anointment will have been watching the behaviour, attitudes, and personality growth of the person whom they have appointed.

There comes a time, especially if you are working in a group, when you are expected to be able to aid the workings of your group or temple, more in order to further the common good of the group as a whole than to obtain a merely personal advantage. You must show that your knowledge is not just superficial vanity, but that you really *understand* what you profess to know; you must ensure that you assist the weaker members of your order by helping to advance their studies with practical help and understanding, and that you do not, by ignorance, folly or stupidity disgrace yourself and others, and by so doing, bring *all* into disrepute. You should by then be above the petty power struggles that so often take place in the opening grades of most occult orders: they are the bane of any esoteric school. So many fine groups, orders and schools have been brought crashing down in ruins through this, simply because their members have not been able to rise above the situation and realize its higher potential. In consequence everything ends in ashes and the aspirants are merely left with a bitter taste in the mouth.

Other Uses of Anointment

An excellent description of the anointing oil is given by Maimonides in the *Moreh Nevochim*, where he writes: 'The anointing oil produced a twofold benefit: the pleasantness of what was anointed with it, and the dignity and sanctity of that which was separated by it from the rest of its kind, and consecrated to a more excellent use, whether it were a man,

or a garment, or any utensil.' Anointing must not be
thought of as suitable only for people, for amulets and
talismans were also anointed in the belief that it made them
more effective, as were swords, wands, rings and temple
equipment. So many items benefit by the consecration of
anointment. The prophets anointed the ring finger of the
left hand, in the still popular belief that this finger had a
direct connection with the heart. The anointing of the sick
was a frequent practice amongst the Jews, as it was with
many other nations. Its use is advocated in the New
Testament (James 5:14)

The use and custom of anointing the dead at burial was a
common practice. When the disciples murmured against
the woman for 'wasting' an alabaster box of spikenard, by
breaking it and pouring on the head of Christ, He
admonished them saying 'She is come aforehand to anoint
my body to the burying.' (Mark 14:8). He further expressed
His approval of the act by saying that wherever the gospel is
preached, 'this also that she hath done shall be spoken of for
a memorial of her.' (Mark 14:9). Christ was either
anointed, and buried in the manner of the Jews (John
19:40), or, according to the other three gospels, the
annointing was to be done later. His name is *Christos* in
Greek – 'the Anointed One', for he combined in one body
and person – King, High Priest and Prophet. He said 'The
Spirit of the Lord is upon me, because he hath anointed me
to preach the gospel to the poor.' (Luke 4:18.)

Egyptian Anointing Ceremonies

Many of the bodies and mummies of the ancient Egyptians
were buried with an anointing tablet, which consisted of an
alabaster tablet with seven hollows to contain the seven holy
anointing oils. Its purpose, according to ancient Egyptian
occult practices, was to provide magical protection to the
deceased on their journey to the next world. The Egyptians
also placed cones of odoriferous ointments in their hair, so
that it gradually melted with the heat, anointing their
bodies with sweet oils. The anointing of kings has been with
us as far back as ancient Egypt, and it may even be older
than that. The now famous back panel of the throne,
discovered in the tomb of Tutankhamen, shows the young
king being anointed by his queen.

Coronation Anointing

Anointing is a most important part of the British coronation ceremony, which is the time when the Ampulla and Anointing Spoon are used. An ampulla is a small vessel with a round body and a narrow neck, which was used for holding oil and perfumes, used by the Greeks and Romans for toilet purposes, though the Ampulla of the British Crown is in the shape of an eagle. The oil used at the Coronation is said to contain the oils of Cinnamon, Jasmine, Rose, with Ambergris, Benzoin, Civet and Musk, which would be a very beautiful compound giving a very rich fragrance.

Simple Anointing Oils

Another compound consists of the usual base of pure Olive Oil into which you add Myrrh, Cinnamon and Galangal. A simple oil said to be used sometimes by the Roman church consists of Olive Oil and Balsam.

An oil you may find useful is a *sabbat anointing oil*, compounded of Balm of Gilead, Saffron, Cinquefoil and Verbena, suggested ratios, in the same order, being $1 + \frac{1}{4} + 1 + 1 + 20$ parts of vegetable oil (which can be used instead of Olive Oil, though as Olive Oil is sacred to the Goddess of Wisdom, Minerva, many people prefer to use it.) Do not be afraid to experiment with the oils and ratios for yourself.

If you wish a bath for Purification, to which herbs are usually added in a muslin bag, try this purificatory bath oil, compounded of Hyssop, Lavender, Valerian, Verbena: use a ratio of $1 + \frac{1}{2} + \frac{1}{2} + \frac{1}{2} + 20$ parts of Almond Oil, though the Almond Oil *must* be the sweet Almond Oil and *not* the bitter. About a dessertspoonful or tablespoonful should be enough, but this can vary according to preferences. This is pleasant before any ritual, and should definitely be used before any *serious* ritual. The oils should be stored in real crystal, at least glass, *never plastic*. Use a crystal container or phial if possible, and if it has a silver stopper, so much the better. But crystal is the thing to aim for, so do try.

CHAPTER FOUR

THE ALTAR OF INCENSE, THURIBLES, CENSERS AND BOATS

Although this chapter is primarily concerned with the burning of incense, the various items used, and the Altar of Incense, let us take a brief look at altars in general.

The world altar is derived from the Latin *altus*, meaning 'high, and thus 'exalted' (this is, after all, the main principle behind the concept). It usually signified an elevated place, or a raised platform on which the sacrifices or rites of the Gods were performed. It was on this 'high place' that offerings were made, and whence they were supposed to ascend to the Most High, consumed by fire. This led to the further supposition that the higher the altar was placed, the nearer it approached the Most High. In many cases it was located in the high mountains.

Among the Jews the altar was the place where the worshipper presented his gifts and devotions, and where God recorded his name and manifested His Prescence. It was the place where the pious offered their devotions both public, domestic and private. With the coming of the Tabernacle, when it was finally established in the land of Canaan, two altars were erected, both having specific measurements and material construction, with rules as to their use.

Origins of Altars

It would be hard for any writer or researcher to state a time when the use of altars first came into being, and what prompted it. There is little doubt that the conception has been with Man for a very long time. There can be little argument that it acted as a focal point for the suppliant, and even more so if many were gathered together. It gave a centre of orientation for the whole ritual, just as the hub of a wheel holds the wheel together: every part is drawn towards, and depends on, this centre. If the hub of the wheel is broken, then the whole thing just falls apart, for there is nothing to hold it together. In any act of vandalism, desecration, or destruction of *any* Holy Place, no matter who is responsible, the culprits will always make for the altar. All things revolve around the altar, and evolve from it. It is the centre of all, whether it is within a building, or erected outside, in either a constructed, or a natural place. The altar has the effect and purpose of signifying the 'focal point', and helps the participants to concentrate, so that any Force evoked does not dissipate itself through lack of clarity, and provides a clearly defined area or working space – in much the same way as an artist defines the limits of his work with the size of his canvas or frame.

An altar is, astrologically speaking, very much like the action of the planet Saturn, which 'defines the limits and boundaries'. While it is true the altar acts as a focal point, we do not wish to give the impression that it is essential. There are certain rituals where an altar is not necessary, the 'clearly defined space' is determined by the perimeter of the Magical Circle, among other methods. The first altars were quite often simply mounds of earth, or natural, flat rocks, which are two of the things that come under the rulership of Saturn. Later they were created artificially from wood, and perhaps, finally, from polished stones.

Many descriptions of these primitive forms of altar can be found; many of them were round, some are square, and others were rectangular. Although they differed greatly in height, the one thing they usually had in common was the fact that they faced the east, or the rising sun. In ancient Druidism it was considered impious to turn your back on the sun. Mountains that were considered sacred were approached from the west so that the worshippers, while ascending the mountain, were climbing to face the eastern, rising, sun. We still adhere to this custom by entering churches from the west to the east, where the altar is placed. At times, in certain parts of the creed, we bow towards the east, which is a survival of bowing to the sun.

The Function of Incense

Let us now come back to the methods of burning incense in church, temple or home practice. Incense has proved to be one of the most popular ingredients of any ritual practice. Its use has, however, caused some dispute, not only among the established church bodies in the past, but also among some ritualists. Some argue that it forms a major part of the ritual and is therefore given prominence with other ritual practices.

The other school of thought does not subscribe to this view. This holds that the use of incense should be a 'background' one, unobtrusive in operation and only noted because of the resulting smoke, sweet or otherwise, depending on the type of ritual being operated. There are no hard and fast rules with regard to these two *seemingly* opposed opinions. The matter is one of personal choice, and depends on the type of ritual being worked as to whether it is prominent or unobtrusive. If you are being guided by a teacher or school, you will naturally be given instruction in the matter. If you are working on your own, or with a small group by yourselves, you will have to make up your own mind on the method you prefer; as you progress, experience will guide you as to which works *best for you*.

Censers and Thuribles

There seems to be little or no difference between these two items, apart from their etymology. 'Censer' appears to have come through the French into English, while the other, 'thurible', appears to have come from Latin (*turibulus* – a censer), which derives ultimately from the Greek.

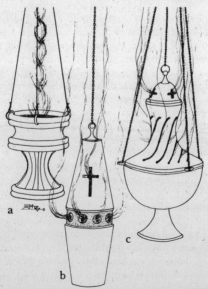

Figure 1. Three examples of thuribles or censers.

Both censers and thuribles are basically portable incense altars, usually hung on chains which can also be used for swinging by hand. Sometimes the person who actually performs the duty of incense is called a censer, or thurifer. The simplest method of burning your incense is in a decorative holder or container, which can, within reason, be made of quite a large range of materials, metal, ceramic, and so forth, which you have filled with sand. The smouldering charcoal generates quite a lot of heat, and if this were placed in *direct* contact with many materials it will crack or damage the container. Hence the risk of fire resulting from carelessness is ever present.

Making an Inexpensive Censer

Attractive ceramic items can be used if they are first filled with sand, but do not fill level with the brim. If you wish you can put a small tin lid on the sand to take the charcoal and the incense. If, however, you put the charcoal directly on to the surface of the sand, do not have the sand level, but make a few scratch marks with a pencil or your finger to allow the air to reach the underside of the charcoal or it may go out. If you do use this method of laying the charcoal and incense on the sand you will have to keep a reserve supply, for eventually you will have to take off the top layer. This will happen when you remove the ashes of the previous burning, especially if the incense last used is not suitable for mixing with the incense you wish to use next.

This cheap alternative to a thurible or censer gives tremendous scope to the imaginative and they should keep their eyes open for suitable containers which can be adapted for this new purpose. A shape appropriate to the ritual being operated or the planet may also be employed – rose-shaped for Venus, for example, a swan or fish-shaped container for Jupiter, and so on. This is, of course, only if you wish to extend the idea, for one container for incense is quite sufficient. It should not be necessary to point out that plastic is best avoided in these suggestions. Florists often have small hanging vases in metal or some ceramic material that can be filled with sand and used, but if they have any drainage you will naturally have to line the container to stop the sand from coming out (see *Figure 1a*).

They often have cords or chains and can be hung from a decorative bracket or a small hook fitted into a ceiling beam. If the cords or chains are too short, however, take

them off and fit new ones. You can adjust the height as you
wish for either artistic appearance, or convenience of use.
Many attractive items can be found that are not
manufactured for hanging in this way, but if you attempt it
carefully, holes can be drilled to adapt them for this
purpose. This item also makes an excellent temple light,
that can be either hung or carried. If you decide to change
the cords, or chains because they are too short for use,
purple, gold or silver coloured cords are excellent
alternatives. Purple (or mauve) is the colour of the planet
Jupiter, ruler, among other things, of religion and religious
philosophies in general. Gold (or orange), is the colour of
the sun, and the Archangel Michael, while silver (or white)
relates to the moon and the Archangel Gabriel, Angel of the
Annunciation. This applies equally to censers and lights.

Sand

I usually take my sand from the sea-shore, and, if damp, it
can be put in a plastic bag to be dried, preferably in the
Sun, either on a tray or newspaper. This has the added
symbolism of the element of earth having been washed by
the element of water, the sea, the 'Mother of Life'. It is best
taken, if possible, from a spot where few people have been
trampling around, or just after the ebbing of the tide when
the sand has been washed clean with the sea water.

Making a Thurible

Many people are skilled with their hands, so there is no
reason why they cannot make their own thurible or censer
for their own or group use. There is the added bonus of it
being consecrated by personal effort. There was a time
when it was considered essential for a ritualist or a magician
to make every piece of the equipment that he would use,
and many schools still insist on this practice. Most thuribles
are made of brass, but there is no reason why other, much
cheaper, materials cannot be used. I am thinking here
particularly of mild steel (some church thuribles are being
made of this now). Steel and iron are acceptable
alternatives to brass, and all are under the rulership of the
planet Mars, one of the fire planets. Incense, it may be
noted, is very often used to represent the element of fire in
ritual practice.

The thurible mainly consists of three parts. The
decorative outer casing consists of a base and lid, the latter

having decorative perforations, not only to allow the smoke of the incense to get out at the top but also to allow the air to get in, for without this the charcoal will die for lack of oxygen and go out. Inside is set another container, to act as a liner in the base of the thurible, and this is generally made of a heavy guage material to take the burning charcoal and incense. It is normally hung on three chains, which are attached by three rings to the lower container and fixed. These three chains are also fitted to a circular plate at the top of the thurible which has a ring attached to it for hanging on a stand or bracket. This we could call the suspension plate. The lid has three rings attached to it on the lower edges, through which the three hanging chains freely pass, so that it can slide up and down. A fourth chain is usually fitted to the top of the lid, and this passes freely through a large hole in the suspension plate. It normally has a large ring fitted on the end, so that when the ring is pulled the lid is raised, riding up on the three suspension chains. This serves the purpose of raising the lid to charge the thurible with charcoal and incense before or during the ritual, if necessary. It also serves to remove the inner liner to clean the thurible of the exhausted materials (see *Figure 1c*).

Some thuribles are made without a base and with a round bottom to ensure that the person using it, the thurifer, can only put the thurible on to its bracket or stand. It does become very hot with use, and the stand or bracket is the safest place for it to be. This is why it is best given to the care of one person only, who has the sole task of its operation, its care and safety.

Keeping the Incense Burning

If you watch a good thurifer you will notice that he, or she (for quite often in the past it was the 'Temple Maidens' who performed this task), occasionally lifts the lid of the thurible up and down, thus causing a very slight down-draught. This allows more air to get to the incense and keep it alive during the ritual and assists the burning. This is often done by suspending the thurible on one of the fingers, and putting the thumb or one finger in the 'lid-ring' to raise the lid up and down. Don't worry if this makes the chains rattle, for this is as much a part of the ritual as all the other attendant noises.

The amount of incense you burn depends on the size of the room being used and the number of people that will be attending. A 'dry run' is useful, unless you are familiar with the room; after all, you do not want so much smoke that you need a guide dog to find the altar. Better to err on the side of scarcity than over-abundance. With incense it is easier to add more than to take away from what you have. Do not get carried away when using a thurible by giving a virtuoso display of incense 'acrobatics', for very few people are experienced enough for that kind of performance. For one thing, it is very dangerous.

Keep the chains of the thurible fairly taut to stop them getting in a tangle. In fact, some modern thuribles only have two chains to prevent this problem, one for hanging, the other for raising the lid. Now there is also a single chain model: it supports the thurible and the single chain goes through the lid which you lift by hand, or in an alternative design the single chain just supports the thurible, which is of an open design to permit charging (see *Figure 1b*).

Keep the thurible in front of you in procession to prevent it getting caught and spilling. Swing the thurible through about forty-five degrees: that will be quite enough to direct the incense to where it is required. When all is needed is 'background' incense, put the thurible on its stand or bracket and 'stoke up' from there if need be.

Making a Censer

A pattern for a censer, which you may like to construct, consists of a simple tube of metal (see *Figure 2*). You can also use a square design (instead of round), and there may even be some strong tins of round or square shape with lids that you can adapt by taking off the bottom. Most modern tin openers cut very closely and neatly and any roughness can be filed smooth. You will have to put feet on the bottom to raise the censer and allow the free entry of air to keep the charcoal and incense alight. These can perhaps be cut from the metal bottom that you have removed, if you are doing it this way. Fix the legs with self-tapping screws or small nuts and bolts. The legs can be straight, right-angled or curved, simple or elaborate – the style is up to you and should be in keeping with your intended design. Perhaps three legs for the circular design, and, naturally, four for the square.

Each side of the square design could have a different symbolism or design, which could be turned to the front to face the ritualist, depending on the ritual being operated. Designs could represent the four seasons, four elements,

THE ALTAR OF INCENSE

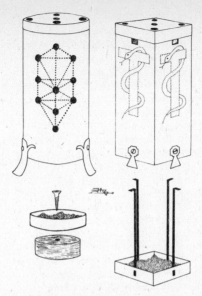

Figure 2. Making a censer.

four phases of the moon, and so on. The circular design
could take two, or three designs at the most. For the
incense, one method is to suspend the 'pan' inside the body.
This can be a lid, slightly smaller for air circulation, square
or round according the shape of the body of the censer. It
can be hung by three wires for the circular, and four wires
or strips for the square type (see *Figure 2*). Make it strong.
Holes are drilled in the sides of the pan to take the
suspension wires and make the pan a deep one, or as deep
as you can. You can also put sand in the pan to act as a heat
insulator if you wish.

Put the wire through the holes drilled and turn them up
with plenty of wire to spare. Close the wire tight with pliers
so they will not come out (you can twist the wire for safety,
but soldering is better). The suspension wires are then cut
according to how low you want it to be in the body of the
censer. This is usually lower than the 'smoke holes',
otherwise no incense smoke will emerge from them.

Make your designs and drill them first so you will be able
to decide on the length of the suspension wires in relation to
them afterwards. The wires are then bent to a deep hook to

fit over the top rim of the body and, naturally, they must all
be of the same length, or the incense pan will not be level.
You may have to cut small slots into the top rim of the body
to take these wires or the lid will not fit. If, however, you use
a slightly larger lid for the top of the body, this will not be
necessary. The other alternative for the incense pan is to
obtain your lid (square or round, and, as before, slightly
smaller than the outer casing) and, with a single screw in
the centre of the pan, screw the lid to a circular or square
piece of wood of the appropriate height. Make the base
fairly large so that it will not tip over. This also acts as heat
insulation for the hot pan (though this will be negligible if
you use sand as a base in the pan). Light your incense in the
pan and lower the outer casing over it when it is burning.
This method means that the pan is not fitted to the censer
casing as in the first method, so it will have to remain in the
position throughout the ritual. You can fit handles to the
outer casing of the type that uses the pan suspended inside,
but it has to be carried with care. Make the pan very deep,
and remember that, though this type could be considered
portable, it is *never* swung. You may have to drill holes in the
lid at the tope of your censer, but be sure to give it a test run
before you do this as it may not be needed.

Decoration

Finally, when you are satisfied with your censer, you can
finish it off with heat-resistant paint. Colour is a personal
choice, but a simple black or your planetary colour would
be suitable. If you decide to adapt a commercial tin for the
body of your censer, and there is no reason why you should
not, remember to remove any original paint before you
cover it with the colour of your choice.

Adaption of existing materials is a very commendable
practice and great ingenuity can be exercised, but we must
still aim at as high a standard as we can within such
limitations. The size, height, and so on, are matters of
personal taste, and the size of the room, altar and other
furnishings will have to be taken into account when you
decide on the scale. This is the reason for omitting any
measurements on the designs given in this book which you
can adapt to your own requirements. Anyone with patience
can, with varying sizes of drills, make a most effective and
symbolic pattern or design. Put it on the metal with wax
pencil or crayon before drilling. A most effective 'Tree of

Life' glyph could be used, using a large drill for the ten *Sephirah*, and a smaller drill for the 'Paths' (this is shown and suggested in the design of the round censer in *Figure 2*). Other suggestions are a Tau Cross (*Figure 2* shows a form of this with a snake around it on two sides of the square censer), a Greek or Balanced Cross, the Fleur-de-Lys, Sun and Moon design – the possibilities are endless, but the most important thing is to choose the symbolism that is important to you, or your group.

I have suggested that the top of the censer should have a lid to prevent the smoke emerging as from a chimney and rendering the patterns that you have drilled in the side of the censer quite useless. Incense coming out of these designs, especially the 'Tree of Life' glyph, can be most effective, and if the censer is flanked by two (or even more if you wish) temple lights it may even prove useful as a meditational aid or as a stimulant for imagination and assist those who possess clairvoyant faculties. It is often of great benefit to throw colours (with the aid of coloured lights) appropriate to the Ritual or Power invoked onto the incense smoke. Some may regard this as a little theatrical, and while it is true that this ought to be done and affected by the imagination, anything which assists this is desirable. Quite often aids to the development of the will and imagination can be discarded at a later date, but do not disdain factors that will assist you to gain the desired mastery and skills. Try not to be wholly dependent on them and, use them with the view of their final removal.

Decorating Censer Lids

If holes are desired or are necessary in the lid you can make a design to suit yourself, or you may care to use the one suggested in *Figure 2*, which is very simple and has excellent symbolism. The five holes drilled in this manner represent the Greek, or Balanced Cross, or, as it is often called by Occultists, the 'Balanced Cross of the Cosmic Creator'. The four outer holes can be said to represent the four cardinal points of the compass, the four seasons, the 'Four Pillars of the Earth', and so on, with the central hole the 'seed' or germ of potential or manifested life.

Five is the number of the Major Arcana, 'The Hierophant or Pope' in the Tarot. This often represents religion, philosophy, exoteric knowledge or 'that which is given out', as opposed to the 'High Priestess', who symbolizes the Mysteries, secrecy, or 'that which is not given out or revealed', esoteric knowledge. You can see how symbolism is a frutiful 'seam' to work: one discovery leads on so swiftly to another. The five in this form can often be seen in some church processions; the thurifer (the one), swinging his thurible goes first while behind him are three people (the three), walking abreast, the centre one bearing aloft the processional crucifix, the symbol of the faith, flanked on either side by two people bearing processional lights, and, behind these three, the priest or high priest.

It may be advisable as we have suggested to stand your censer on something, in case any hot charcoal spills or splutters over. There are many pleasing heat-proof mats that are adequate for this purpose, and many may even have an appropriate design of flowers, herbs and so on. A ceramic tile with felt stuck to the base can also be used if you think it is necessary.

An incense 'boat' is literally shaped like a boat which comes to a point at both ends. It has a half lid which lets the incense out, and allows for charging or cleaning. It usually has a heavy base to help prevent accidental tipping over, and is normally supplied with a spoon for the incense. It can vary in length from approximately $3\frac{1}{2}$ to $6\frac{1}{2}$ inches (9cm to 17cm).

Altar of Incense

The two altars, the Altar of Burnt Offerings and of Incense, and the Table of Shewbread of the Tabernacle, are described twice in the Bible, in Exodus. The first mention comes in Exodus 27:1 for the Altar of Burnt Offerings, and Exodus 30:1 for the Altar of Incense. The second time they are both mentioned is in Exodus 37:25 and 38:1, where the whole matter of the furnishings of the tabernacle is dealt with.

What we are going to suggest here is that as a great deal of the Western Mysteries Tradition leans heavily upon Jewish symbolism (Qabbalah, Hebrew, alphabet, names, etc.), a small working model of the original Altar of Incense makes an excellent substitute for the more traditional thurible or censer in use in church or temple. This altar stood before the veil of the Holy of Holies, behind which was the Mercy Seat on the Ark of the Covenant. This altar was taken into the Holy of Holies once a year, on the Day of Atonement – 'and bring it within the vail; and he shall put the incense upon the fire before the Lord, that the cloud of the incense may cover the mercy seat that is upon the testimony.' (Leviticus 16:13). It is a design that is not used much in ritual work. A small one can be constructed in the manner of a censer as mentioned in the previous examples and used in a similar manner. It is not a hard design to copy and it does look most effective when it is made up. It has the advantage of being different from the more usual patterns.

The measurements given in the Scriptures make it follow the 'four-square – double cube' concept, saying – 'the length of it shall be one cubit, and the breadth of it a cubit; it was foursquare; and two cubits was the height of it.' It is reasonably certain that there was more than one type of cubit in use in Biblical times, and there were possibly two different measures having this description at least. One was from the elbow to the wrist, while the other was a handbreadth longer. The Hebrew, like the Latin term *cubitus*, signifies the 'forearm'. One of these, many claim, was known as the 'common' cubit of man (Deut. 3:11), considered to be twenty-two inches, and the other as the 'sacred' – eighteen inches.

Measurements

The largest concensus of opinion favours a cubit of eighteen inches, and by this reckoning, the Altar of Incense must be eighteen inches square by thirty-six inches high. What matters more in my opinion, than any argument about the length of the cubit, is that the ratio was one by one square, by two high, which is maintained no matter what the actual measurements may prove to be. If you decided that you were going to make a small altar, to stand in your temple, and your 'cubit' were three inches, then your altar would be three inches square and six inches high. If you decided, on the other hand, to use this item as a more or less permanent piece of temple furniture, you may choose a measurement of eighteen inches square and thirty-six high, or two foot square by four foot high, and so on. *Figure 3* shows the construction of the altar while *Figure 4* shows the design made up (measurements have been omitted from the diagrams for this reason: the ratio is fixed, the measurements are personal according to your needs).

Materials

The original Altar of Incense was made of shittim wood.

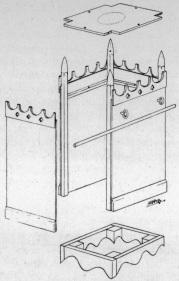

Figure 3. Construction of the Altar of Incense

Figure 4. The completed Altar of Incense.

The shittah tree is cited once in the Bible, 'I will plant in the wilderness the cedar, the shittah tree, and the myrtle, and the oil tree.' (Isaiah 41:19.) It should be noted from this passage that this tree was considered worthy of planting with the myrtle and other fragrant shrubs. The wood of this tree is mentioned many times in the Hebraic form of *shittim*, which is the plural form of *shittah*. This is, in later translations or revised versions given as acacia (or *Acacia arabica, Acacia nilotica* or *Acacia seyal*). This is a very beautiful closely grained wood which tends to darken with age and has the extra advantage of not being attacked by insects. The fact that so many parts of the tabernacle were made from this type of wood while the Israelites were wandering in the wilderness seems sufficient evidence that the wood in question could not be, as has been conjected by some, a valuable foreign wood, but of the few timber trees native to the desert where the Israelites were wandering. It was fairly widespread in Egypt, and we find in Numbers 33:49, 'and they pitched by Jordan, from Beth-jesimoth, even unto Abel-shittim in the plains of Moab', the last encampment of Israel before crossing over the Jordan. 'Abel-shittim' is translated as 'meadows of the acacias'.

Make this altar of wood therefore, and do not paint it, at least not all over. Leave the natural graining in keeping with the original concept. This could be of oak, cedar, mahogany – or even acacia wood! One or two coats of varnish will bring out the grain and protect the wood from dirt. If, however, you use woods like plywood or chipboard which have little or no real grain, perhaps it may be better to apply a coat of primer and then paint or spray the whole altar gold. In the Biblical descriptions, there was a 'crown of gold' around the top and the 'four horns' were also covered in gold. Beneath the crown, were placed two rings of gold, upon the two sides and by the two corners, 'to be places for the staves to bear it withall'. You can make the gold decoration from good quality gold paint, while some good stationers or art stores have a supply of genuine gold leaf, used for putting letters or decoration on books, which is excellent, though a little expensive. You could just cover some parts of the altar with gold leaf – the crown, the horns, and perhaps the ends of the carrying staves. You could cut out an appropriate symbol or motif to stick on the side of your altar, which would be quite sufficient (there are many decorative motifs for whitewood furniture that would serve

for this). I would regard the crown and horns as the most
important part of the altar for this special kind of treatment.

Construction

You will see from Figures 3 and 4 that it is quite a simple
construction. It can be built with very little skill or tools, the
wood could even be purchased pre-cut to size. The altar
consists of four sides, which are fixed to four batons of
wood, glued and/or pinned with panel pins of the
appropriate size. If they are fitted together in the order
shown in the diagram, the thickness of the wood will be
incorporated and accounted for and the shape remain
square. The four batons extend higher than the crown, and
these are shaped to represent the four horns of the altar.

Inside the body we place a shelf to take the incense pan.
The height of this shelf can be adjusted according to the
depth or type of pan you choose and whether you wish to
place it low in the altar (so that it will not be seen) or high.
There are many circular or square stainless steel dishes on
sale today which would be excellent for the job. The size
depends on the size of the altar. A hole of appropriate size
and shape can be cut in the shelf in which this dish could
rest. The use of sand in the dish will act as a heat insulator.
A decorative strip can be stuck around the base and under
the crown. Many highly decorative wood mouldings are
available today: you could even pick out the design with
coloured paints before fitting, though this is a matter of
personal taste. Screw rings are easily obtainable for
screwing into the sides of the altar to take the carrying
staves, and these can be painted gold. The size of the screw
rings you use depends on the size of the altar you are
making, as will the size of the staves that go through them.
The staves should be made for the altar even though they
were probably originally removed when the altar was set in
place (you can leave them in the rings if you wish). Once
you have made the basic altar you can make it as decorative
or leave it as plain and simple as you wish; the main thing is
the basic design of the body, crown, horns and carrying
staves in the proportions given in the Scriptures. You will
have made, in simple construction or otherwise, depending
on your skills, an Altar of Incense that has been used for
many thousands of years, and, according to the Scriptures,
one whose form has been dictated and designed by God.

CHAPTER FIVE

INGREDIENTS

It was realized after this part of the work was started that, unless held in check, it could take on almost encyclopaedic proportions, as the ingredients that are still used in incense, perfumes and anointing oils are so many and varied. So it was decided to try and give as much information as possible in a highly condensed form regarding the type of ingredients that go into the various compounds. Experience has proved that if the reader is pointed in the right direction he will make the journey himself for what he *really* wants to know.

Some of the ingredients have been enlarged upon, while others have been given under a general heading, e.g. herbs, seeds, leaves, gums, etc. So many gums, resins, oils, barks, seeds, herbs and spices have, at one time or another, been combined by Man into a 'suffumigation' or some type of incense. Even today the potential for experimenting has not been exhausted by any means. One of the main aims of this book is to encourage this in the reader.

Raw Materials and Correspondences

Agrimony to Saturn; Bay to the Sun, sometimes Jupiter; Euphorbia to Mars; Eyebright to the Sun, occasionally to Venus or Mercury; Fennel to Mercury, occasionally the Moon; Galangal Root to Jupiter, some authorities say Mars; Grains of Paradise to Jupiter; Lavender, to Jupiter, though sometimes to Mercury; Marjoram to Mercury; Oak to Jupiter, though sometimes to the Sun; Orris to the Sun, sometimes Jupiter; Peppermint to Venus, sometimes to the Moon; Rhus Aromatica, mainly to Mercury; Rosemary usually to the Moon; Rue to Saturn; St John's Wort (Hypericum) to Mercury; Southernwood to Mercury; Valerian to Saturn, some say Mercury; Verbena to Venus,

possibly Mercury; Willow, Witch Hazel and Wormwood,
all to the Moon.

Oils and Spices

Almond to Venus; Ambergris to the Sun; Aniseed to
Mercury; Cassia to the Sun, sometimes given to Mercury;
Civet to Saturn; Ginger to Mars, possibly the Sun; Khol, as
this is a mineral, possibly to Saturn; Lemon and Lime to
Mercury; Mace to Mercury; Mandarin to the Sun; Musk to
Saturn, though some give it to the Sign of Scorpio; Nutmeg
to Venus, possibly to Mercury; Patchouli to Mars in his
Sign of Scorpio; Saffron to the Sun or Jupiter; Sandalwood
(White) to the Moon, but sometimes to Mercury;
Sandalwood (Red) to Venus in her Sign of Taurus; Ylang
Ylang to the Moon or Neptune.

Gums, Resins and Balsams

Gum Acacia to the Sun; Gum Asafoetida to Saturn; Gum
Copal to Jupiter; Gum Dammar to Mercury; Gum Elemi to
Venus; Galbanum to Jupiter; Gum Karaya to the Moon;
Olibanum to the Moon, often the Sun; Opopanax to Mars,
possibly his Sign of Scorpio; Scammony Resin, from the
Greater Bindweed Root, to Saturn; Storax to Mercury
usually, thought sometimes to Saturn; Gum Tragacanth to
Mercury; Gum Thus to Saturn.

   Blue Incense: compounded of Roses and Violets; *Green
Incense*: compounded of Benzoin, Mace and Storax; *Purple
Incense*: compounded of Saffron, Cinnamon and Red
Sanders; *Scarlet Incense*: compounded of Balm, Ambergris,
Grains of Paradise and Saffron; *White Incense*: compounded
of Camphor, Amber, Aloes, White Sandalwood and
Cucumber Seeds.

Signs of the Zodiac

Aries: Myrrh, Lignum Aloes, or a compound of Myrrh,
Hellebore and Cypress. *Taurus*: Pepperwort, Saffron; or a
compound of Sandalwood, Pepperwort and Bergamot.
Gemini: Mastic, Cinnamon, or a compound of Galbanum,
Mace and Mastic. *Cancer*: Camphor, Myrtle, or a
compound of Red Storax, Opopanax and Camphor. *Leo*:
Frankincense, Mastic; or a compound of Myrrh, Juniper
Berries and Frankincense. *Virgo*: Sandalwood, Cinnamon,
or a compound of Pepperwort, Cloves and Benjamin. *Libra*:
Galbanum, Saffron, or a compound of Mastic, Galbanum

and Lignum Aloes. *Scorpio*: Opopanax, Lignum Aloes; or a compound of Camphor, Lignum Aloes and Opopanax. *Sagittarius*: Lignum Aloes, Nutmeg; or a compound of Myrrh, Cloves and Lignum Aloes. *Capricorn*: Pepperwort, Benjamin; or a compound of Sandalwood, Violet Root or Benjamin. *Aquarius*: Euphorbium, Pepperwort; or a compound of Mastic, Mandrake Root and Euphorbium. *Pisces*: Red Storax, Nutmeg; or a compound of Camphor, Red Storax and Opopanax.

Days of the Week
Incenses for the days are suggested as: *Sunday*: Mastic. *Monday*: Myrtle. *Tuesday*: Lignum Aloes. *Wednesday*: Cinnamon. *Thursday*: Nutmeg. *Friday*: Saffron. *Saturday*: Pepperwort.

What do you do if there are no correspondences for an ingredient given? Most people who supply ingredients know the correspondences for the ingredients they supply, if not, you will have to try and assess the correspondences for yourself. In time you will also acquire experience in deciding such matters. Given next is a very condensed list from an earlier work, suggesting certain keywords for the seven planets we use, the seven planets of old astrology.

Astrological Keywords
Sun: Authoritative; bright; dignity; honour; lordly; majestic; regal; stately; warm: glorious odours.
Moon: Alluring; dreamy; feminine; maternal; moist; nocturnal; slumber; receptive: sweet fresh and feminine odours.
Mars: Active; aggressive; caustic; energetic; fiery; penetrating; reckless; urgent: hot pungent odours.
Mercury: Alert; adaptive; busy; dual; lively; nervous; quick; versatile: fugitive odours.
Jupiter: Aristocratic; benevolent; comfortable; ecclesiastical; luxurious; noble; rich; prosperous: generous odours.
Venus: Agreeable; amorous; elegant; frivolous; genteel; indulgent; loving; peaceful; soothing: voluptuous odours.
Saturn: Austere; conservative; doleful; inert; old; prudent; profound; responsible; sober: heavy earthy odours.

We use similar terms everyday in our description of things or situations. We say that a building has a feeling of 'nobility and dignity' which is seen as well as felt. We often assess intangibles or feelings in this way to give them concrete expression, as with the odour of perfumes. Hence many of the fanciful names given to commercial products, like 'Taboo', or 'Primitive', and so on, are all designed to conjure up, supposedly, the right state of mind or feelings. For example, if an odour or perfume suggests to you the Saturnian qualities of austerity, earthiness or sobriety, then this is the scent of Saturn as far as *you* are concerned, for the stimulated response and associated ideas are *personal to you*. This rule applies equally to all other perfumes.

Suppliers and Utensils

If you simply buy a compounded incense for a specific use, and there is no reason why you should not, then this question will not arise, for having found a reliable supplier for your needs, you will order in accordance with your requirements. There are some very good suppliers on the market. It was decided not to include a list of suppliers for the simple reason that omission may be regarded as criticism and could also be unfair. Many magazines have advertisements of suppliers of occult materials, and in this do not neglect what could be called the 'smaller' magazines. These are often run by enthusiasts and a stamped addressed envelope to the editorial office often proves quite helpful.

The main utensils for mixing are a glass, plastic or wooden bowl and wood-spoons, something that can be washed, so the previous mixing will not add to new incense being made. Better keep the utensils for this apart and do *not* be tempted to use your usual kitchen bowls or utensils. Keep oils and resins out of the kitchen away from food.

Testing Ingredients

If you decide to make a stock of ingredients, have a testing session with your ingredients to help you assess their particular quality. Ingredients are best placed on waxed paper. Burn a *tiny* amount of the ingredient on the charcoal, wafting the smoke to your nostrils with your hand. Start with a small amount and increase it if required, especially with any new or unknown ingredient. Test slowly, and increase the amount little by little. Some ingredients give generous odours from small amounts, while others need a much greater amount for a similar effect. You will find that you soon begin to develop a 'nose' for incense. Keep a notebook for your observations, perhaps devising a 'star' system of marking to assess your judgement. Is an ingredient warm, heavy, light, pleasant, sensual, etc? Remember, it is your own personal response that is important, for no two people will react the same to the results of this most subtle art. The faint waft of perfume can stimulate in one person the most pleasant associations of places, occasions, people or a particular person, while to another the same perfume can arouse the most unpleasant memories and feelings.

A small salt or mustard spoon could be adopted as a unit of measure for these tests, while a small set of kitchen spoon measures make excellent graded measures and are easily obtainable. You may find that some ingredients will give excellent results with just one measure, while others may require two, three, or even six. This will help you to assess the 'strength' of ingredients when compounding future incenses.

Start by mixing small amounts of the ingredients together in equal amounts. If you are mixing three ingredients together you may find the greatest response comes from one half measure of the first, one of the second and three of the third. It is wise to write down the combination and amounts in your notebook for future reference. You may hit upon the correct combination immediately, or it may take time, but it will come. This is why quite often only the ingredients of an incense are given to enable the user to adjust the parts to suit his personal taste. This is also why one solar incense, for example, may seem quite different from another, even through the basic ingredients are the same, the compound can be adjusted by varying the amounts, or strength, of one or other of the ingredients to suit personal requirements or taste. When experimenting in this way, do not neglect to use herbs that you would normally think of using in the kitchen. Try rosemary, marjoram, all-spice, or a piece of bark of cinnamon.

Creation Through Correspondences
One thing the beginner often ponders over is how to begin creating an incense for himself. Once more we are faced with the vexed question of correspondences which are, in the main, astrological. If you have knowledge of astrology you will have a firm basis to build on. Lists will follow suggesting a few correspondences of the various sources to

start you off. I do recommend that you add basic astrology
to your skills, if you do not already have some knowledge of
this art. Personally, I could not operate this or many other
occult crafts without astrology, for so much stems from it.
Let us take the headings from some old works and add
further suggestions as to how the beginner may start to
compound an incense based upon these astrological
correspondences.

Francis Barrett tells us, ' ... further we are to be provided
with lights, perfumes, ungents, and medicines,
compounded according to the nature of the spirit and
planet; which agree with the spirit by reason of their
natural and celestial virtue.' (*The Magus*, Book 2.)

1. 'Should the object be to develop a strong personality
and to attract others towards you, especially of the
opposite sex.'

If you are male, use the ingredients of the Sun or Mars,
either separately or together, to which you could add the
ingredients of Aries and/or Leo. If female, use the
ingredients of the Moon and/or Venus, the odours of
Cancer and/or Libra and Taurus. If a little 'feminine
mystery' is felt to be needed, add the odours of Pisces
and/or Neptune.

2. 'Those who wish to have clear and prophetic dreams,
to attempt to dream true.'

Any odours of the Moon, helped by the odours of Cancer,
those of Neptune and the Sign of Pisces. You can add Ash
Tree seeds, or perhaps Bay Leaves.

3. 'To strengthen the health vibrations and to ward off
disease.'

Use the odours of the Sun, as the Sun rules a healthy
body as a complete organism and the heart and spine in
particular. Mars rules vigour, the bodily strength to fight
disease, and the blood. The diet, hygiene and the general
health of the person is ruled by Mercury. Each planet and
sign rules a part of the body and the organs (any book on
astrology will supply this information). You could add
ingredients according to the sign and planet ruling the part
of the body that you feel needs attention or you feel is weak.
Make the odours of Mercury (perhaps Virgo) the basis of
any incense dealing with health matters.

4. 'For the betterment of, or gains in, the financial
conditions.'

Primarily the concern of Jupiter, as Jupiter is the main

INGREDIENTS   55

significator, among other things, of wealth. Jupiter is the
'Greater Fortune' and Venus the 'Lesser Fortune'. Venus is
also the natural ruler of the second house in the horoscope
chart, 'of finances and moveable possessions', and the
natural sign of this house is Taurus, whose odours may be
added to those above.

5. 'For luck and safe travel on any journey that you may
undertake.'

The main significator of travel is the planet Mercury, to
which could be added the odours of his sign of Gemini. Both
the planet and sign are the natural rulers of the third house
of travel and short journeys in the horoscope. Travel abroad
to foreign parts is held to be ruled by the house opposing the
third – the ninth, whose natural ruler is Jupiter and his sign
of Sagittarius, so these odours may also prove effective.

6. 'For success in games of hazard or chance, from which
gain is hoped for.'

Some of the remarks for 4 apply here, but it may be better
to use the odours of Jupiter to which you can add the odours
of the Sun and those of his sign Leo, for these two, the Sun
and Leo, are the natural rulers of the fifth house of the
horoscope, which rules, among other things, all matters of
speculation and luck in general.

7. 'For honours, preferments, and the seeking of favour
from those in power, or of high position.'

The two planets that rule 'men of authority' are the Sun
and Jupiter. The Sun is the ruler of kings, queens, princes
and royalty, presidents, etc. Jupiter has a similar
significance as both are 'royal' planets. Jupiter rules knights
and peers of the realm, especially those in high office in the
Church and the Law, judges, and the Lord High
Chancellor. So use the Sun and Leo and their odours and
perfumes, and those of Jupiter and Sagittarius.

8. 'To bring about success in all undertakings, in
business matters in general, and the commencement of any
new enterprise.'

Mercury deals with commerce in general, and business
accumen. The planets for success are the Sun and Jupiter,
and to a lesser extent, Venus. If the business is dealing with
the public at large, this is the Moon and her Sign of Cancer.
For beginnings and the initiatory force of a business and
most other things, perhaps a touch of Mars. So the above
could read 'To bring about success in all undertakings
(Sun/Jupiter), in business matters generally (Mercury),

and the commencement of any new enterprise (Mars).' The odours of the Moon would be optional.

9. 'If friendship and love be desired, and when you wish your friendship and love to be reciprocated.'

Venus and her odours are associated with peace, harmony, love and marriage, and partnerships of all kinds. Venus, and her Sign of Libra, is the natural ruler of the seventh house of the horoscope, which has, among other things under her rulership, partnership, marriage, and the social aspects of life. Perhaps you could add a little of the odours of the other sign she rules, Taurus.

10. 'To strengthen the mind for the purpose of study, for developing concentration, and for acquiring knowledge in any form.'

The acquisition of knowledge and education in general are the domain of the third house of the horoscope chart. Therefore, the odours of the natural ruler of this house and his sign, Mercury and Gemini, can be compounded. However, what is generally termed the 'higher' or philosophical nature, especially as regards Law or religious philosophy, comes under the domain of the ninth house, its natural ruler Jupiter and his sign of Sagittarius, whose odours may be used seperately or added. Mars would add then the energy to work (not too much), while a little of Saturn, the control and perseverance.

11. 'If it is desired to overcome your enemies and rivals, and to be secure from malice or enmity.'

Mars is the 'fighting' planet, giving both the will and strength to protect what you have, to attain that which you want, and to defend the things you have and yourself, to this you can add any of the odours of his sign of Aries.

The above reasoning may be extended to any compound you wish to make, for any situation. Combine the astrological ruler of the ingredient, with the signs of the zodiac that they rule and their ingredients, and you will have a reasonably reliable basis with which to experiment. Now let us take a look at some of the ingredients that make up incenses, oils, etc.

Ambergris

This is a fatty substance which resembles wax. It is found in the intestines and stomach of the sperm whale. It is used in perfumery as a fixative. Although Ambergris is basically intestinal matter, it is not thought to be the result of any kind of disease, but rather as the pathological product of an otherwise normal stomach or intestine.

Aloes – Lign-Aloes

A very well-known exotic plant, a genus of African plants of the family, *Liliaceae* distinguished by their long fleshy leaves. The juice of the leaves is extracted by bruising, or the gum is taken from the Aloe by incision. The drug commonly known as Aloes taken from this plant is used medicinally as a powerful cathartic. The gum was used a great deal in the embalming of bodies, and mixed mostly with myrrh. The same ingredient may produce the perfume mentioned by this name in the Bible. 'I have perfumed my bed with myrrh, aloes, and cinnamon. Come, let us take our fill of love until the morning.' (Proverbs 7:17). Lign aloes are referred to only once in the Bible: 'As the tree of lign aloes which the Lord hath planted.' (Numbers 24:6.) It has been suggested that this is a Syrian Aloe and not the Indian. It has been accepted as being identical with the 'eaglewood' or *Aquilaria agallochum*. Perfumers, having taken off the bark, used the wood (in Latin *lignum*) to give consistency to perfumes that were too liquid or thin. Of the family of Aloes, the Socratine is held to be the best, deriving its name from the island of Socotra which lies in the mouth of the Red Sea. It is thought that this was the source of the supply of much of the aloes gum, used by ancient priests and embalmers, especially the Egyptians, who make great use of it.

Balm of Gilead

It seems that this may appear under the name of 'Balm of Mecca' also. It is a golden-coloured oleo-resin, which is extruded from the tree, *Balsamodendron gileadense*, or the *B. opobalsamum*. There appears to be another source that comes from America, from the tree, *Icica carana*, but this is held to be inferior.

Bay

Name applied to various species of laurel, *Laurus*, and some other plants. The 'Victor's Laurel' of the ancients was the sweet bay, *Laurus nobilis*, a native of Southern Europe. Its aromatic, evergreen leaves are used for flavouring and cooking.

Benzoin

Benzoin, or Gum Benjamin, is a resin which is obtained by making incisions in the bark of the tree, *Styrax benzoin*, which is native to the East Indies. It has a very fragrant aroma, and is used in the preparation of perfumes, cosmetics, and, naturally, incenses.

Camphire

King Solomon likened his beloved to a 'cluster of camphire'. (Song of Solomon 1:14.). Camphire is one of the earliest known of the spices and perfumes. It is extensively cultivated in Egypt, even today. It is renowned as the dye known as 'Henna' in the East and was used as a dye for the beard, nails, and so on. The nails of many Egyptian mummies were found to have still retained the dye after many thousands of years. The leaves and young twigs are ground to a powder and mixed with hot water to a paste, giving an orange/red hue. The colour can be changed to black by the addition of a preparation of indigo. It was especially prized by the women of Egypt.

Camphor

This is an aromatic, volatile substance obtained from the Camphor tree, *Cinnamomum camphora*, a member of the *Lauraceae*, which is native to South China, Formosa and Japan. The Camphor is distilled from chips of wood of the root, trunk, and branches, which are exposed to the action of steam and afterwards refined. It is used for medicinal purposes and imparts to many of these products a very familiar smell.

Cassia

This is the bark of a plant, *Cinnamomum cassia*, of the family *Lauraceae*. It is an aromatic, and closely resembles the true Cinnamon, for which it is largely used as a substitute. It was often called by Europeans (who obtained the Indian and Arabic varieties) Indian Orris Root, because of the claimed similarity of odour. It was often burnt in temples and in private homes as an incense. The Greeks and Romans obtained their Cinnamon and Cassia from the Phoenicians, deeming Cassia the better of the two.

Charcoal

The charcoal used is usually of willow. It is purchased in

blocks that are square or round, though charcoal powder and granules can be bought. Two types are usually available from commercial outlets: one has an additive (usually saltpetre) to assist burning; the other does not. Some people prefer the latter, although it is slower to ignite because it does not splutter. Sometimes it is suggested that saltpetre (potassium nitrate) is added to the incense itself, to compound what is generally termed 'self-lighting' incense. In my view this is an undesirable practice. Saltpetre is, without any doubt, under the rulership of the planet Mars because it is an ingredient of gunpowder. when used to give 'quick-lighting' it is erratic and it has a rather acrid smell when burning. This is why, if it is to be used, it should only be added to the charcoal, which is fired before adding the incense, not to the incense itself. This would be, in effect, adding the vibrations of Mars to every incense you compound and this obviously, is not desirable. If you wish to make the charcoal without the additive easier to light, add *a small amount* of methylated or surgical spirit. There are other additives that can be used, but some of these are dangerous and are best avoided.

The whole secret of using your charcoal and incense lies in the seemingly contradictory rule: You must burn your incense without *burning* your incense.

By this we mean you do not have your charcoal burning intensely. Having it too hot, or red hot, just drives off the essential oils without having the desired effect; it turns the gums and resins to ash; and, most of all, it is *very* uneconomical. You will be surprised how much incense smoke can be obtained from just a pinch of incense when the charcoal is burning properly. It is best to light the edges of the charcoal and let it ignite slowly, even when you are using the type with the additive, which I personally prefer. The charcoal will *appear* to be still black, even when fully ignited, with some red spots at the edges. Put on your incense and let the charcoal do the rest. Simply remember the above golden rule. An old pair of tweezers to hold the charcoal while you light it is ideal, as is an odd 'blow' now and then. Lay the charcoal in the pan, just add a drop of spirit (if required), and ignite.

If you are unable to get the prepared charcoal, an alternative I have found useful is the charcoal granules used in barbeque grills. It can be used as it is or crushed into powder and made into blocks. It will have to have a binding agent which can be the white of an egg (good symbolism there), or perhaps Gum Arabic or Tragacanth. Mix into a fairly stiff paste, spread into a shallow tray and leave to dry thoroughly. If the surface of the slab is lightly scored into convenient squares (like a chocolate bar), it will break more easily when dry.

Cinnamon

Another bark of a tree, *Cinnamomum zeylanicum*, which is also a member of the family, *Lauraceae*, and is grown in Ceylon, Java, Brazil and the West Indies, etc. Oil of Cinnamon is obtained from the inner bark, and is used both as a flavouring and in medicine, to which it imparts another of those familiar aromas.

Cinquefoil

Genus of plants, *Potentilla*, belonging to the family, *Rosaceae*, the typical species *Potentilla reptans* is a creeping perennial, widely distributed throughout the British Isles, growing in pastures, meadows and on banks.

Copal (Gum)

Of Mexican origin, a fragrant, translucent white resin distilled from *Copalquahuitl*, Mexican Copalli incense. It was originally found in Mexico, but is now found in Zanzibar, West Africa, Mozambique, Madagascar and India.

Dammar (Gum)

A Malayan resin from the genus *Dammara*. This may possibly prove to be a collective name for quite a variety of resins obtained from different trees growing in the East Indies and New Guinea. A point of interest is that Dammars were once used for caulking ships. White Dammar is from the genus, *Valaria indica*, while the Black Dammar is from the genus *Canarium strictum*.

Elemi (Gum)

Although the word 'elemi' appears in Virgo's Latin *Practica*, which was printed in Rome c.1517, the use of the word appears to be modern. Elemi Oil is known as 'Elemin'. It is obtained from the tree *Canarium commune*, from Manilla, the *Icica Icicariba*, from Brazil, and the *Elaphium elemiferum* from Mexico.

Frankincense

This surely, must be accepted as one of the most popular and famous, free-burning resins in the world. It was one of the three gifts of great value, gold, frankincense and myrrh, that the three Magi brought to Bethlehem to give to the new born Jesus. One gave gold for 'kingship', the second gave frankincense for 'holiness', while the third gave myrrh, symbolic of suffering and death on earth. It is mentioned many times in the Bible, especially in connection with the Holy Temples and Places, and as a fumigation at animal sacrifices. It is a resinous product, which is obtained by peeling off a thin layer of the bark of the tree, which is done slowly so that the resin flows from the inner wood. It is of the *Burseraceae* family, of the genus *Boswellia thurifera*, a native of Africa, India and Arabia. The *libanum* of the ancients is frankincense, and the Hebrew is *lebonah*. It does not always appear under this name in incense. It is also called *Olibanum* or *Gum Thus*, which are the same thing. This is a resin that can safely be substituted for any other resin or gum, and it can be used on its own for *any* ritual or invocation. A most versatile ingredient, acceptable to all, and an ingredient to have in plentiful supply. In passing, though, it has to be mentioned that its use was not always limited to incenses. In Gerard's *Herbal* we find that frankincense, and mastic, are two of the ingredients used in a cure 'that taketh away the old ache in the huckle bones called Sciatica'.

Galbanum

This ingredient appears but once in the Biblical account, as one of the ingredients of the Holy Incense. (Exodus 30:34). As Galbanum is rather pungent, it may seem strange to many that it should appear as a choice of a 'perfume' that was to be made of 'sweet spices'. Pliny tells us, however, that the reason for its inclusion in perfumes was to make them retain their fragrance for a longer time. (*Natural History* 8:2). It was further believed by the older writers that the smoke of Galbanum was a very effective defence against gnats and serpents, which it drove away. It has always been used as an ingredient in medicine, and although its existence has been known for quite a long time, there is still some disagreement as to the plant from which it is obtained. According to some it is the, *Bubon galbaniferum*, to others the *Ferula galbaniflua*, from which a milky white juice flows when

cut, which soon hardens to the air. The rendering of the
Hebrew word *chalenah* is derived from a root meaning
'milky or fat'. The odour of Galbanum is pungent and
rather strong, though many do not consider it unpleasant.
It has medicinal properties which are similar to Asafoetida,
which is taken from it. It consists of gum, a resin, a volatile
oil with a trace of acid. One of its uses today is in the
manufacture of varnish.

Heliotrope
Plant of the *Boraginaceae* family, Heliotropium genus of
plants, a few of which are found in Europe. The forked
spikes, of blue, white or lilac flowers, and also the leaves,
alter their position constantly so as to face the Sun. The
garden heliotrope, *Heliotropum arborescens*, was introduced
into Europe from Peru.

Hellebore
Plants of the *Ranunculaceae* family. The Green Hellebore, or
'bear's foot', flowers in early spring with pale yellowish-
green flowers. 'Stinking Hellebore', produces a flower stem
up to a foot in height, with drooping pale green flowers.

Henbane
Wild plant, *Hyoscyamus niger*, common on waste ground in
England, Central and Southern Europe, and Western Asia.
A branching plant, one to four feet high, it has hairy leaves
and a somewhat nauseous smell. The yellow flowers are
bell-shaped. It is sometimes grown for medicinal purposes,
but *its use is dangerous*.

Jasmine
Jasmine, or Jessamine, genus of plants *Jassminum*, of the
Oleaceae family, found in many parts of the world, but
mainly in the East. Jasmine Oil is used in perfumery. The
common Jasmine, *Jasminum officinale*, a native of Persia and
Northern India, but naturalized in Europe, is a climber
growing over twelve feet high, bearing clusters of white or
yellow, sweet-smelling flowers. The Chinese Winter
Jasmine, *Jasminum midiflorum*, produces brilliant yellow
flowers before its leaves appear and is found in America.

Khus-Khus
Vetiver, or Khus-Khus, is a fragrantly scented root of a type

of Indian grass. The Hindus weave it into grass mats, which they hang over doors and windows. By keeping the mat damp, the air is cooled before it enters the house.

Honeysuckle

Popular name for the plants of the genus, *Lonicera*, of the *Caprifoliaceae* family. The common English Honeysuckle, or Woodbine, the *Lonicera periclymenum*, is a climbing plant with sweet-scented flowers, purple and yellow tinted outside, and creamy white, inside. The North American Trumpet Honeysuckle, the *Lonicera sempervirens*, is very handsome, including scarlet and yellow varieties.

Mace *see* **Nutmeg**

Mandrake

This has been the subject of superstition since very early times, and folk-lore tells us that this is an aphrodisiac and fertility herb. The Arabs call mandrakes 'Devil's Apples'. This attribute is borne out in the Biblical account of Rachael (Genesis 30:1.). The idea derives from the fact that the roots often resemble the human form, a characteristic often depicted in many old drawings of the plant. The Mandrake is called botanically *Mandragona officinarum* and belongs to the family *Solanaceae*, which also includes Belladonna, Henbane, Thorn-apple and Tobacco. Like many of its relatives, the Mandrake is a narcotic, the root containing an alkaloid similar to atropine. It is often described in older works as a pain-killer and, an 'inducer of sleep'.

Mastic

The Mastic tree, *Pistacia lentiscus*, is a fairly common sight in Mediterranean areas, in the Holy Land. The gum resin is obtained by the familiar, bark incision method. It is often used as a means to help sweeten the breath and there are many who think the act of chewing or masticating gave the tree its name. The wood bark and fruit emit a very pleasing odour when burnt.

Mint

An aromatic plant of the genus *Mentha* in the family *Labiatae*, widely distributed in the temperate regions.

Garden Mint, *Mentha viridis*, and Peppermint, *Mentha piperita*, are best known.

Myrrh
One of the best known of the perfumes, perhaps along with Frankincense, with which it is often associated. As it was also an ingredient of medicine, it was one of the earliest articles of commerce, highly prized by the Egyptians, Jews, Greeks and Romans, as it still is to the present day. It is mentioned frequently in the Bible and it is most likely that several kinds of Myrrh were known, one being the *Balsamodendron myrrha*. It was found in Arabia, and its extensive use in embalming, as well as in perfumes and incense, suggests its correspondence with Saturn, as does its symbolic representation of 'suffering' and of the dead. Classical legend tells us that Adonis was born from a Myrrh tree which, after a ten month gestation, burst its bark to let the beautiful infant emerge. His mother is said to have been a woman called Myrrh and that she had been turned into a Myrrh tree soon after she had conceived the child, so it is not surprising to find Myrrh being offered at the Festival of Adonis.

Myrtle
Myrtle enjoys its reputation as a result of its rich green leaves which, in season, are highly contrasted with the white, star-like clusters of flowers, which fill the air around with a very agreeable fragrance. It was commanded by law that the Israelites should dwell, during the Feast of the Tabernacles, in huts or 'booths' made of the branches of the Myrtle, the Olive and the Pine. (Nehemiah 8:14.) The Lord said 'I will plant in the wilderness the cedar, the shittah tree, and the myrtle.' (Isaiah 41:19). 'Instead of the thorn shall come up the fir tree, and instead of the brier shall come up the myrtle tree.' (Isaiah 55:13). The vision of Zechariah took place among 'myrtle trees that were in the bottom', where he saw 'a man riding upon a red horse.' (Zechariah 1:8). Myrtle, *Myrtus communis*, is still used as a spice and the whole of the dried plant is used in Syria for perfumery.

Olibanum *see* Frankincense

Nutmeg
The kernel of the seed of the evergreen tree *Myristica fragrans*, native to the Moluccas. Both the nut and its secondary covering, known as Mace, are used as a spice in cookery.

Olive
Of all the trees in the Bible and in the works of ancient authors, none is more frequently mentioned than the Olive Tree. No other tree was more highly honoured by the nations of old. It is one of the earliest specified plants in the Bible, being beaten into first place by the fig. It was an Olive branch that the dove brings back to Noah, to show that all was well once more and that the waters were subsiding, both Olive and dove being emblems of peace among the civilized nations of the world. To 'offer the Oliver branch' meant that you wanted peace. It is a symbol of trust and mercy, (Psalms 52:8). It is said that they yield the best type of oil if plucked or are carefully shaken off by hand before they are fully ripe (Isaiah 17:6 and 24:13), and not thrown into the press. It was called Omphacinum, or the 'oil of unripe olives', and also 'beaten' or 'fresh oil'. Sometimes the oil was trodden out by the feet, and these types of press were called *gath-shemen*, hence the name of Gethsemene, the garden situated at the foot of the Mount of Olives. The finest oil was used for the basis of anointing oils, being prepared with fragrant spices, and as this oil is also attributable to Minerva, the Goddess of Wisdom. For the temple light, this fine 'beaten' oil was to be used: 'pure oil olive beaten for the light, to cause the lamp to burn always.' (Exodus 27:20).

Onycha
Meaning 'nail' or 'claw'. This is one of the ingredients of the Holy Incense of Exodus, and this is understood to be the horny operculum, or shell, of a species of shellfish. In Latin it is called, *Ungala aromatica* or *Unguis oderatus*. Discorides 'it is the cover of a shellfish, like the purple, and it is found in the spikenard lakes of India, and it doth give forth a sweet odour, for that the shellfishes there do feed on spikenard. The best is brought from the Red Sea, white and fat. Some out of Babylon, which is blackish, is burnt for sweet savour.' He further quotes Maimonides as saying it is the nail or shell which men used to put in perfume. Another point of

view differing from this one claims that Onycha is a Rock
Rose, *Cistus landaniferus*, which produces a gum called
Labdanum. As said above, the Greek word Onycha means
a nail or claw, so it is suggested that the markings on the
petals probably gave rise to the name, while others further
suggest that the Onycha in the Holy Incense of Exodus may
have derived from Styrax.

Orris Root
The underground stem of a species of Iris grown in
Southern Europe. It is violet scented, and is used in
perfumes.

Pepper
This is a climbing plant of the East Indies, the *Piper nigrum*.
Black pepper is produced by gathering the berries when
they are green and crushing them; for white pepper the
berries used are ripening and turning red; the much hotter
Cayenne Pepper is made from the berries of a variety from
tropical America, *Capsicum fastigiatum*.

Rue
A shrubby plant, *Ruta*, of the family *Rutaceae*, native of
Southern Europe and temperate Asia. Common Rue, *Ruta
graveolens*, formerly called 'Herb of Grace', was much used
in mediaeval medicine.

Saffron
Mentioned in the 'Song of Solomon', Saffron, *Crocus sativus*,
native of Asia Minor, is similar to the purple crocus. The
part of the plant used is the stigma which gives a distinctive,
aromatic odour. It is used as a flavouring and colouring
ingredient, and it has been used in medicines. It is not a
very cheap ingredient to use, but when you consider that
the stigma of four thousand blooms go to make an ounce,
this is not surprising. Dried marigold petals may be
substituted.

Salt
Salt was an indispensable commodity to ancient peoples. It
is difficult for us to imagine its importance to our ancestors.
It is a known fact, apart from certain medical conditions
where its use is reduced or precluded, that salt is essential
for health, vigour and well-being. It has been used since

earliest times as a condiment for food – 'can that which is unsavoury be eaten without salt?' (Job 6:6.) It was mixed with the fodder for cattle as an antidote against the effects of the heat of the climate. Salt found great acceptance among the Hebrew worshippers. All meat offerings were required to be seasoned with salt. As salt was important it was sold in large quantities in the Temple market and a large quantity was kept in a special chamber, assigned for its storage, in the Temple itself. They had an inexhaustible supply of this commodity on the southern shores of the 'Salt Sea' (Genesis 14:3), now called the Dead Sea.

Christ told His disciples, 'Ye are the salt of the earth: but if the salt have lost his savour, wherewith shall it be salted? It is thenceforth good for nothing, but to be cast out, and to be trodden under foot of men.' (Matthew 5:13). He further tells us, 'For every one shall be salted with fire, and every sacrifice shall be salted with salt. Salt is good: but if the salt have lost his saltness, wherewith will ye season it? Have salt in yourselves, and have peace one with another.' (Mark 9:49).

Holy water should have some grains of 'blessed salt' mixed with it to be truly effective. Stoups or basins have been built into the entrances of churches since Norman times in which is placed the water/salt mixture blessed by the priest. Those entering the church dipped their fingers into this water and salt and sprinkled themselves with it as a symbol of purification.

These illustrations given here show the importance in which salt was, and still is, held. With the discontinuance of the 'burnt-offering' and the greater use of incense in its place, salt was, and is, sometimes added to the incense itself. Bearing in mind the properties of sterility and barrenness associated with a surplus of this 'element', only a few grains are needed to flavour. As salt is a 'creature of the Earth' it may added with good effect to any incense of that particular element, though a few grains may well add 'savour' to other types of incense if you feel so inclined. I have never seen any definite ruling on the matter, though I am sure that many practitioners have strong views, or otherwise, on its use or omission. Sea-salt is easily obtained today, the coarse-grained for the salt-mill being the best because it is pure and, unlike the fine varieties, it has no additives to assist its 'free-running'.

Spikenard

This is a very famous perfume of the East, was very expensive and considered to be 'very precious'. (John 12:3 and Mark 14:3). It is also known by the name of *nard* (Hebrew), and *nardos* (Greek), its name in Greek (*nardostchys*) meaning 'ear of wheat', referring to the shape of the flowers. It has many spikes from one root, hence its name, and these appear like a 'tail of ermine'. It is usually accepted that the more valuable variety is that of Indian origin, *Sinbul Hindhi*, a rich red ointment with a most fragrant odour. The word ointment incidentally is applied to various preparations of oil and perfumes, and also refers to the compound of medical ingredients that we know and use today. Spikenard was much in use for anointing the head, especially by the Romans.

Stacte (Storax)

This Greek word was generally assumed to mean a gum that distills from Myrrh. Moses spoke of *nataph*, which has a literal translation of 'liquid drop'. This word has also been rendered as *neteph*, which has been translated as 'Stacte'. Incisions made in the branches of the *Storax officinalis* causes the liquid resin to flow and this later hardens. It is one of the ingredients of the Holy Incense to be burnt on the golden Altar of Incense. It is also used in incenses of the Roman Catholic church today.

Sulphur

Known from ancient times, Sulphur is pale yellow and odourless until burned. It is brittle, solid and insoluble in water. It is widely distributed as an element in volcanic regions, and frequently used in the manufacture of many items, including sulphuric acid, chemicals, explosives, dyes, and drugs.

Tobacco

A narcotic plant of the genus *Nicotiana*, and of the family *Solanaceae*, whose dried leaves are prepared for chewing, smoking, and snuff. Often used to induce trance states, and, strange though it may seem, it is sometimes used in incenses. From the Churchwarden's accounts of St Peter's, Barnstaple in 1741: 'Paid for tobacco and frankincense burnt in the church – 2/6d.'

Verbena

Genus of plants of the *Verbenaceae* family, having large tubular flowers arranged in close spikes. Colours range from white to rose, violet to purple. There are about one hundred species, mostly in the American tropics. Lemon-scented Verbena, *Lippia citriodora*, belongs to the same family.

Wormwood

Whenever Wormwood is mentioned in the Biblical text it is always in the context of 'bitterness', and there are many references to it. Several species of Wormwood, of the genus *Artemisia*, are to be found. It is one of the ingredients of the liqueur Absinth – Latin and French name for Wormwood is *Absinthium* and *Absinthe*. This bitterness does not prevent certain species having valuable medicinal properties. One type grows in England, *Artemisia vulgaris*, or Common Mugwort. In Revelation we find a Star called Wormwood, which fell from heaven at the sounding of the Third Angel. Its purpose may have been to destroy, by bitterness or poison, and not by fire, famine or the sword: 'And the third part of the waters became wormwood; and many men died of the waters, because they were made bitter.' (Revelation 8:11). The herbs were often steeped in wine to counteract the possible effects of alcohol.

Woodbase

A rather fine name for sawdust! Many ritualists and others disdain and even condemn its use. While it is admitted that the gums and resins are highly desirable, they seem to forget that the burning of odoriferous woods were used *before* these items by many nations. Pliny tells us that in post-Homeric times 'people know only the smell of cedar and citrus as it arose in volumes of smoke from the sacrifice'. Wood can be used in many incenses, along with many other items of the vegetable kingdom. In many cases it may have been used by people unable to afford the more expensive ingredients, as wood was cheaper. It must not be forgotten that woods have the same planetary rulerships as the more expensive ingredients. The use of woodbase could be considerably improved by the simple expedient of not using just *any* woodbase, but a woodbase appropriate to the incense being compounded. After all, making sawdust is easy enough for anyone. As a guide the following is given,

though some duplication will be found in the lists because of
differing opinions; these are given to show other points of
view.

Sun: Bay; Palm; Walnut; Ash; Citrus. *Moon*: Willow;
Ash; trees abounding in sap or having an affinity with
water. *Mars*: Pine; Hawthorn; those that are prickly and
thorny. *Mercury*: Nut-bearing trees (not necessarily edible);
Myrtle; Pomegranate; Hazelnut; Mulberry. *Jupiter*: Birch;
Vines; Fig; Oak; Olive; Lime; Maple; Fir. *Venus*: Apple;
Fig; Elder; Plum; Peach; Alder; Birch; Pear; Sycamore.
Saturn: Pine; Yew; Elm; Beech; Cyprus; Ivy; Poplar;
Quince.

You may find that other lists disagree with some of the
above. Remember, it is a general list. A further guide, taken
from an earlier work, may prove useful at this point.

Soft woods come under the Moon and Venus; hard woods
under Mars and Saturn; the woods called 'redwoods' for Mars;
expensive and rare woods for the Sun and Jupiter; Rosewoods
(genuine), under Venus; the 'blackwoods' under Saturn;
Walnut to the Sun; and those that are commonly called
'yellow-woods' for Mercury and the Sun; Woods that are called
'white or cream-woods', e.g. Ash, come under the Moon. It is a
matter of combining the guidelines given to decide the
rulership of any particular wood you are seeking.

The following is a condensed list of many of the items you
will find in lists of incenses, anointing oils, etc. By
combining the lists together, you will find that Rosemary
for example is a herb, with medicinal uses, cosmetic uses,
culinary use, and can also be used as a herb tea, while Rue,
is a herb with medicinal use.

Herbs
Agrimony; Bay-leaf; Basil; Daminana; Euphorbia;
Eyebright; Fennel; Henbane; Hyssop; Marjoram; Maté
Tea; Peppermint; Rosemary; Rue; St John's Wort; Vervain;
Wormwood/Absinthe.

Flowers
Chamomile; Lavender; Orange; Rose (Rose-hip syrup can
often be substituted for this).

Seeds
Aniseed; Coriander; Grains of Paradise; Pimentoes.

Leaf
Bay; Henna; Verbena.

Spices
Cayenne; Cinnamon; Cloves; Garlic; Ginger; Mace;
Nutmeg; Paprika; Saffron.

Oils
Almond (Bitter and Sweet): Aniseed; Calamus; Cassia;
Camphor; Cedarwood; Cinnamon; Clove; Eucalyptus;
Lemon; Lime; Mandarin; Olive Oil; Patchouli; Rosemary;
Stephanotis; Vertiver; Winter-green; Ylang-ylang.

Mineral
Brimstone; Khol; Sulphur.

Perfume Ingredients
Almond; Ambergris; Calamus; Cassia; Cedarwood;
Cinnamon; Civet; Coumarin; Ginger; Heliotrope; Lemon;
Lime; Mandarin; Musk; Patchouli; Stephanotis; Ylang-
ylang.

Animal By-Products
Ambergris; Civet; Musk.

Roots
Galangal; Ginseng; Licorice; Mandrake; Orris; Rue;
Aromatica; Valerian.

Barks
Cassia; Oak; Cedar; Aspen; Cypress; Willow; Witchhazel;
Yew; Myrtle; Larch.

Balsams, Gums and Resins
Acacia; Aloes; Asafoetida; Benzoin; Galbanum; Karaya;
Labdanum; Mastic; Myrrh; Olibanum/Frankincense/
Thus; Oak Moss; Opopanax; Storax; Tragacanth;
Dragon's Blood; Scammony.

Culinary Uses
Aniseed; Basil; Bay-Leaf; Cassia; Cayenne; Coriander;
Fennel; Garlic; Ginger; Grains of Paradise; Juniper;
Lemon; Lime; Licorice; Mace; Marjoram; Mandarin;
Nutmeg; Olive Oil; Paprika; Pimentoes; Rosemary;
Saffron.

Medical Uses
Agrimony; Brimstone; Camphor; Cinnamon; Clove;
Eucalyptus; Euphorbia; Eyebright; Fennel; Ginseng;
Henbane; Hyssop; Licorice; Menthol; Rosemary; Rue; St
John's Wort; Sulphur; Valerian; Vervain; Wintergreen;
Wormwood.

Cosmetic Uses
Almond; Chamomile; Cinnamon; Henna; Khol; Lavender;
Lemon; Lime; Mandarin; Olive Oil; Orris; Patchouli;
Rose; Rosemary; Sandalwood; Verbena; Witch-hazel.

Herb Teas
Basil; Chamomile; Fennel; Maté; Orange (best added to
non-herbal tea); Peppermint; Rosemary; Valerian (not too
pleasant).

CHAPTER SIX

INCENSE FORMULAS

Formulas

In this part of the work you will find the recipes or formulas for your incenses; there are enough of these to start you off on this very rewarding path. As I have said elsewhere, you will find that the quantities are not always given, for within the framework provided, there is plenty of scope for personal preferences. In Solar Incenses for instance, I personally prefer the strong smell of orange, whereas you may not like this as much. Try to remember to keep the peel and the seeds from any fruit and vegetables you may have; these can be dried, ground and stored for future use with your incense.

The combination that you or your group prefer is not one that can be taught by reading books, even this one, it has to be worked out for yourselves by work and experience. There is no other way! More often than not, if you provide set recipes it gives the false impression that this is how it *has* to be done, and it may also mean that people will not be encouraged to experiment with their own ideas. Even the recipes that suggest specific portions can be varied by you, and why not? After all, that is how they were arrived at and determined in the first place.

The use of synthetic ingredients often causes the beginner some concern. It is of course better to use the natural ingredients but, if this is not possible, I see no reason for not using the synthetic ones. Many of these are derived from a coal-tar base, e.g. diphenyl oxide for geranium, cinnamonic aldehyde for cassia, and so on. There is no reason why only the expensive, and sometimes rare, traditional perfumes should be the only ones employed in magic and incenses. Today there is a vast selection of reasonably priced synthetic fragrances which will serve the same purpose for all, save the purist. Those who have clairvoyant ability record that burning incense has a 'figure of eight' aura which is in 'rapid convolution'. When synthetic materials

were likewise viewed, it was recorded that the movement
was much faster, and the colours a little harsher, yet this
need not worry us too much.

Incenses of the Seven Planets

We start with some versions of the incenses of the 'Seven
Planets' of old. The first set given has two versions you can
try. These 'seven' are, perhaps, the most important and
basic of our incense stock. The Seven Planets of old
astrology are the main significators over so much that
happens on the 'earth plane'. They are the 'old Rulers' of
the twelve signs of the Zodiac, and according to some
schools of occultism/astrology, they are still regarded as
such. These seven are concerned with that part of Mankind
which 'decays and dies', and is subjected to the 'changing
fortunes of life', from birth with the Sun and Moon, to
decay and the death of the physical vehicle that ends with
Saturn. Uranus, Neptune and Pluto, in the main, are not
directly concerned with this aspect of Mankind. They are,
basically, concerned with the spiritual or 'inner' nature of
Man which can be indirectly influenced by the physical to
some extent, but which is not moved by the passing phases
of the 'outer' life. The number seven occurs yet again with
the seven trumpets and seals, the seven stars before the
Throne, the seven churches in Asia (Assiah), with their
seven candlesticks, and so on. The correspondences which
return to this number are legion. Mediaeval occultism gives
' ... seven magical Works', classified into the following
groups: Works of Light and Riches; Works of Mystery and
Divination; Works of Science and Skill; Works of
Retribution and Punishment; Works of Love; Works of
Intrigue; and Works of Malediction and Death.

I am not sure if they are still available, but if you can get
them (or perhaps a substitute), herbal dyes are excellent for
adding the correct planetary colours to the appropriate
incenses. This is excellent symbolism, and it has the added
advantage of making the planetary incenses easily
recognizable by their colour. Use orange for the
Sun/Sunday, though the incense of the Moon/Monday
may have to be left in its natural state as white dyes are not
readily available. Red would be the colour to use for
Mars/Tuesday; yellow for Mercury/Wednesday; purple,
mauve or lilac for Jupiter/Thursday; blue for
Venus/Friday, and green for Saturn/Saturday.

The *Table of Planetary Hours* gives the methods of working

out the times given for compounding your incenses. It should also be remembered that it can be used for many other matters, as pointed out later, and is *not* just for use with your incenses.

Sun

Incense 1	*Incense 2*
Gum Arabic	Orange Peel
Olibanum	Heliotrope
Cassia	Sunflower
Orris Root	Laurel
Bay	Cinnamon
Saffron	Acacia Flowers
	Ambergris Oil
	Heliotrope Crystals

Compound on Sunday in the hours of the Sun. Only use the hours of the Sun, or, if it is absolutely necessary, those of a friendly planet on other days. You really must make the effort if you are to achieve anything worthwhile.

Moon

Incense 1	*Incense 2*
Olibanum (Frankincense)	Lign Aloes
Gum Karaya	Ginseng
Artemesia Absinthum (Wormwood)	Jasmine
White Sandalwood	Camphor
Mandrake Root (pref. Female)	Cucumber Seeds
	Ranunculus (Buttercup)
	Ylang-ylang Oil
	Honeysuckle

Compound on Monday in the hours of the Moon

Mars

Incense 1	*Incense 2*
Dragon's Blood Powder	Rue
Black Peppercorns	Opopanax
Absinthe	Siamese Benzoin
Oak	Capsicum (Chilli)
	Geranium

Any hot, spicy substances may be added to either of these incenses, which are to be compounded on Tuesday in the hours of Mars.

Mercury

Incense 1	Incense 2
Gum Tragacanth	Cinnamon
Gum Dammar	Storax
White Sandalwood	Herb Mercury
Mace	Marjoram
Verbena	Aspen
Clove	Lime Flowers
Camomile	Larch
	Lemon Peel

Compound on a Wednesday in the hours of Mercury.

Jupiter

Incense 1	Incense 2
Gum Copal	Florentine Iris (Orris Root)
Cedar	Galbanum
Hyssop	Saffron
Grains of Paradise	Oak
Orris Root	Balm of Gilead or
	Poplar leaves or buds
	Aspen

Compound on Thursday in the hours of Jupiter.

Venus

Incense 1	Incense 2
Gum Benzoin	Lign Aloes
Gum Elemi	Myrtle
Red Sandalwood	Clover
Nutmeg	Marshmallow Herb
Damiana	Mint
Rose	

Compound on Friday in the hours of Venus.

Saturn

Incense 1	Incense 2
Myrrh	Storax
Scammony Resin	Elm
Rue	Yew
Cypress	Musk
Vervain	Civet

Prepare on a Saturday in the hours of Saturn.

Incenses of the Lemegaton

These are prepared in the hours and on the days given above for the 'Incenses of the Seven Planets'.

Sun

Aloeswood	Ambergris
Cinnamon	Cloves
Frankincense	Myrrh
Musk	

Moon

Camphor	Olibanum
Jasmine	Ginseng
Mandrake (pref. female)	Onycha

Mars

Benzoin	Dragon's Blood
Euphorbia	Hellebore Root
Lodestone	Pepper
Sulphur	Tobacco

Mercury

Mace	Mastic
Cinquefoil	Styrax Liquid
White Sandalwood	Storax
Narcissus	Cloves
Artemesia	

Jupiter

Aloeswood	Storax
Cedar	Ash
Lapiz Lazuli	Ambergris

Venus

Ambergris	Galbanum
Coral	Aloeswood
Musk	Benzoin
Myrtle	Storax
Red Sandalwood	Rose

Saturn

Asafoedita	Sulphur
Henbane	Civet
Musk	Galbanum
Mandrake (pref. male)	Scammony

Special Note: The Ingredient *HENBANE* is orally *POISONOUS*.

A further selection of 'suffumigations' for the Seven Planets of old, taken from a very old manuscript, is given here. The

various animal parts have been omitted from the
ingredients. Use the same hours and days indicated earlier.

Sun

Saffron	Myrrh
Aloeswood	Musk (a little)
Wood of Balsam	Ambergris (a little)

Moon

White Poppy	Benjamin
Storax	Camphor (a little)
Lodestone	

Mars

Euphoriba	Root of Hellebore
Bdellium	Powder of Lodestone
Salammoniac	Sulphur (a little)

Mercury

Mastic	Storax
Cloves	Powdered Agate

Jupiter

Seeds of Ash Tree	Storax
A shoot of Olive	Benjamin

Venus

Musk	Dried Red Roses
Ambergris	Red Coral
Aloeswood	

Saturn

Grains of Black Pepper	Powder of Lodestone
Grains of Henbane	Myrrh
Root of Mandrake	

Talismanic Incenses

The incenses listed here with which talismans are 'fumed
for consecration', are taken from the works of Theophrastus
Paracelsus (1493-1541). Talismans should be exposed to
the fumes of the incense on the correct day, in the correct
hours of the planet to whom the talisman is dedicated. (See
Table of Planetary Hours).

Talisman of the Sun: (Solis Dies – Sunday)
Composed of cinnamon, frankincense, saffron, and red
sandalwood, burnt with dried heliotrope stalks and laurel.

Talisman of the Moon: (Lunae Dies – Monday)
Composed of aloes, crushed cucumber seeds, camphor, white sandalwood, burnt with dried stalks of artemesia, ranunculus and selenotrope.

Talisman of Mars: (Martis Dies – Tuesday)
Composed of dried absinthe, black peppercorns, dragon's blood and rue.

Talisman of Mercury: (Mercurii Dies – Wednesday)
Composed of benzoin, mace and storax, burnt with lime flowers, marjoram and narcissi.

Talisman of Jupiter: (Jovis Dies – Thursday)
Composed of ambergris, balsam, cardamon, frankincense, mace, orris root and saffron, burnt with fig, oak, pomegranate seeds and poplar.

Talisman of Venus: (Veneris Dies – Friday)
Composed of musk, roses and violets, burnt with red sandalwood and olive wood.

Talisman of Saturn: (Saturni Dies – Saturday)
Composed of alum, asafoedita, scammony and sulphur, burnt with ash, cypress and black hellebore stalks.

Incenses of the Elementals
An Elemental is a spirit which is evolved, or is evolving in and from, one of the four Elemental Kingdoms. (Modern occultist writers often give a fifth, ether or spirit which is not used here). It is claimed that they have a definite form which can be seen by those with certain clairvoyant ability. Some are regarded as benign, while others are not. Their handling is sometimes regarded as a 'tricky' affair, especially in Geomantic questions and rituals (the realm of the Earth Elementals, or Gnomes.) So it is usually advised to keep Geomantic questions simple and free from any possible ambiguity; if you do not, they usually find a double meaning for themselves and act upon it, giving their answers accordingly. Many regard their attitude as more that of perverse or mischievious children, rather than one of actual malice to Humanity. Because of this many consider

that it is unwise to approach them. Be firm with them at all
times or it will most likely get out of hand, but be courteous
– 'courtesy is the Hallmark of Heaven!'

The Elements of Air are called *Sylphs*, of Fire, *Salamanders*,
of Water, *Undines*, and of Earth, *Gnomes*. It may be well to
mention in passing here, that Man differs in a major aspect
from the Elementals in that *all four Elements* are expressed in
his nature, whereas, by definition, Elementals partake of
only one. It is often held that the Sylphs (Air) are the most
difficult to deal with, and the category of Elementals most
loathe to deal with we crude mortals. However, some
believe the Salamanders (Fire) to be worse.

The twelve signs of the Zodiac are divided among the four
Elements, with each Element presiding over three signs.

The signs of the Zodiac ruled by the Element of Fire are:
Aries (Mars), Leo (Sun), and Sagittarius (Jupiter).

The signs of the Zodiac ruled by the Element of Earth
are: Taurus (Venus), Virgo (Mercury), and Capricorn
(Saturn).

The signs of the Zodiac ruled by the Element of Air are:
Gemini (Mercury), Libra (Venus), and Aquarius
(Saturn/Uranus).

The signs of the Zodiac ruled by the Element of Water
are: Cancer (Moon), Scorpio (Mars/Pluto), and Pisces
(Jupiter/Neptune).

The times to compound your Incenses of the Elementals
are suggested by the above lists. If you are mixing an
Incense of the Undines (Water Element), then you should
use the day of the Moon (Monday and the Moon's hours),
or Tuesday (Mars and his hours), and Thursday (Jupiter
and his hours.) If it is an Incense of the Gnomes (Earth
Element), then you use Wednesday (Mercury and his
hours), Friday (Venus and her hours), or Saturday (in the
hours of Saturn), and so on.

Incense of the Gnomes

Gum Tus	Scammony Resin
Myrrh	Musk
Storax	Cypress
Red Sandalwood	

Incense of the Undines

Gum Karaya	Lign Aloes
Olibanum	Cucumber Seeds
Camphor	Ylang-ylang
Osier (Willow)	Jasmine

Incense of the Sylphs

Gum Elemi	Verbena
Gum Tragacanth	Ash Wood
Gum Dammar	Damiana
Benzoin	White Sandalwood
Mastic	Violet

Incense of the Salamanders

Dragon's Blood	Ginger Root
Galbanum	Labdanum
Gum Copal	Euphorbia
Gum Arabic	Capsicum
Galingal Root	

Incense of Riches and Favour

Benzoin	Aloeswood
Pepperwort	Cloves

Prepare on Sunday and Thursday in the hours of the Sun and Jupiter in those days.

Incense of Success in Business

Benzoin
Cinnamon

Prepare on Sunday, Wednesday and Thursday, in the hours of the Sun, Mercury and Jupiter on those days.

Incense of Abra-Melin

Tears of Olibanum	4 parts
Stacte (Red Storax)	2 parts
Lign Aloes	1 part

Ordinary frankincense may be used in place of Tears of Olibanum. Rose, cedarwood, apple or pine may be substituted for aloes if desired, or if not available.

Incense of Solomon

Aloes	Benjamin
Nutmeg	Musk

Any other fragrant spice, oil or ingredient may be added if you wish. I usually make this up either on a Sunday or a Thursday in the hours of the Sun or Jupiter.

Incense of Pan

Pan, quite rightly, has many incenses created in his name.

His incense is often called 'of lust and seduction'. It has to be very 'earthy, seductive and primitive' or what the old fire and brimstone evangelist would call, 'of the flesh'. I for one have never heard, nor believed the cry 'Pan is dead!' The ingredients given below will produce an excellent incense for Pan. The ingredients in parenthesis may be added, or used as alternatives, and this will allow more choice when making up a compound to suit your own personal taste.

Patchouli Essence/Leaves	
(Scammony)	Vervain (Musk)
Benzoin (Storax)	Olive Oil (Yew)
Pine (Myrrh)	Civet
Wormwood (Mandrake pref. male)	Church Incense – as a base –

You can, if you wish, add a touch of oil of pine, or oil of cloves, or even both. I add a little heavy red wine to this either in the mixing or the incense before using. The best day for mixing this incense is a Thursday, in the hours of Jupiter, under a waxing Moon. Do not use the Full Moon.

Incense of Vehuel

Olibanum	Ambergris (a drop)
Balm of Gilead	Orris Root
Grains of Paradise	Heliotrope

VEHUEL ... 'who presides over the great of this world, but especially over those who are raised and distinguished for their talents and virtues.' Prepare on Sunday or Thursday in the hours of the Sun and Jupiter.

Incenses of the Sabbat's
Spring Equinox/Summer Solstice

Fennel	Cedar
Rue	Geranium
Cinnamon	Penny Royal
Rose	Church Incense
Red Sandalwood	

Autumn Equinox/Winter Solstice

Myrrh	Fir or Pine
Scammony	Solomon's Seal
Storax	Musk
Wormwood	Church Incense
Ivy	

These incenses should be used at the times of the all-important quarterly figures of the Sun's entry into the four Cardinal Signs of Aries, Cancer, Libra and Capricorn. The Spring/Summer Incense is used for the Sun's entry into Aries or the first day of Spring (approx. March 21/22nd), and its entry into Cancer, the longest day (approx. June 21/22nd). The Autumn/Winter Incense is used for the Sun's entry into Libra, the first day of Autumn (approx. September 23rd), and its entry into Capricorn, the shortest day when it is reborn from darkness to bring back the Northern Hemisphere's Spring and Summer (December 21/22nd approx). For the exact days and times you will need to consult an ephemeris, and one would be wise to have the appropriate incense prepared and ready for use at these times.

Egyptian Incense

Camphor	Sulphur
Laurel Leaves	Root of Aromatic Rush
Salt	Myrrh
White Resin	

A good, general incense in the Egyptian style. If you wish to dedicate, or consecrate your incense to a specific Egyptian god or goddess. The following list will offer some guidance. *RA*, on Sunday in the hours of the Sun; *ISIS*, on Monday in the hours of the Moon; *HORUS*, in the hours of Mars on Tuesday; *THOTH TEHUTI*, on Wednesday in the hours of Mercury; *MAAT*, on Thursday in the hours of Jupiter; *HATHOR*, on Friday in the hours of Venus; *ANUBIS*, in the hours of Saturn on his day, Saturday.

Incense of Health

Dammar	Gum Arabic
Olibanum	White Sandalwood

Make up on Wednesday in the hours of Mercury.

Incense of Wealth

Orris Root	Red Sandalwood
Grains of Paradise	Gum Benzoin

Make up on a Thursday in the hours of Jupiter. You could also use Sunday in the hours of the Sun.

Incense of Happiness

Jasmine	Red Sandalwood
Ylang-ylang	Ambergris
Rose	Benzoin

Friday is the best day for compounding this incense, though other days may be used, avoiding the hours of Mars and Saturn – possibly even their days – for safety.

Incense of Exorcism

Calamint	Mint
Peony	Palma Christi Oil

I suggest Tuesday in the hours of Mars for preparing this incense. Saturday in the hours of Uranus is also highly recommended, for when an 'irresistible force' (Uranus), meets an 'immoveable object' you may take it that 'something's got to give!'

Incenses of Success

Incense 1		*Incense 2*	
Sandalwood	25 parts	Frankincense	16 parts
Vertivert	8 parts	Sandalwood	12 parts
Frankincense	8 parts	Myrrh	10 parts
Myrrh	8 parts	Cinnamon	10 parts
Winters Bark	5 parts	Patchouli Leaves	5 parts
		Orris Root	5 parts

Mix well together and compound these incenses on either Sunday or Thursday in the hours of the Sun or Jupiter. (If these hours are genuinely unavailable, you could substitute the hours of Venus).

Incense of Annihilation

This will *not* get rid of a rich uncle, grandmother, or anyone else for that matter. In fact, it is used to banish an 'atmosphere' or 'influences'. One word of advice, if this incense is used as an adjunct to any banishing ritual, make it an out-of-doors one. If you do not accept my advice the first time, you will the second. Perhaps a 'consecrated' clothes-peg for the nose is an alternative! It is best compounded on Saturday in the hours of Saturn/Uranus, or Mars/Pluto. Tuesday proves a · useful alternative day, using the same hours given above.

Gum Asafoedita	Palma Christi Oil
Myrrh	Sulphur
Yew or Cypress	

Incenses of Wrath and Chastisement
Mars Formula

Dragon's Blood	Cayenne
Rue	Ginger
Peppercorns	Sulphur (a pinch)
Olibanum	

Saturn Formula

Scammony	Elder
Storax	Patchouli
Myrrh	Sulphur (a pinch)
Yew or Cypress	

Compound the Mars incense on Tuesday in the hours of Mars. The Saturn incense should be prepared on Saturday in the hours of Saturn.

You can add to the Mars incense a pinch of magnetized iron filings. (You can also add this to the Saturn incense if you wish; the Mars incense, however, is the more important). You can make your own by magnetizing some iron with a magnet and filing some off.

Incenses of Divination

Incense 1	*Incense 2*
St John's Wort	Olibanum
Wormwood	Cloves
Aniseed	Camphor
Valerian	Mastic
Solomon's Seal	Wormwood
Saffron	Cinquefoil
Bay or Ash Seeds/	Bay or Ash Seeds/
Leaves (opt.)	Leaves (opt.)

These are useful incenses to aid your attempts at divination. If you are attempting materialization, Dittany-of-Crete *must* be added (to both), its smoke is a most excellent basis for magical manifestations. Madame Blavatsky said of Dittany, that it was 'the most powerful of all the magical perfumes.'

Simple Incense

Sandalwood	2 parts
Myrrh	1 part

Mix well together, when convenient.

Incense of Love and Attraction

Olibanum	8 parts	Cinnamon	4 parts
Sandalwood	4 parts	Orris Root	2 parts
Rose	4 parts	Sawdust/Woodbase	
Musk	2 parts	or Church incense	15 parts

A sweet and fragrant incense, made up on Friday in the hours of Venus.

Commanding Incense

Cassia	8 parts	Patchouli	4 parts
Orris Root	4 parts	Sandalwood	8 parts
Myrrh	4 parts	Sawdust/Woodbase	
Olibanum	4 parts	or Church Incense	4 parts

This is held to be of Oriental Origin, giving power and authority to those who burnt it. Made up on Sunday or Thursday in the hours of the Sun and Jupiter on those days.

General Incense

Frankincense	10 parts	Basil	2 parts
Myrrh	5 parts	Gum Arabic	2 parts
Rosemary	4 parts	Allspice	2 parts
Marjoram	4 parts	Gum Tragacanth	2 parts

Mix all the above ingredients together, this is an excellent all-round incense that can be used at any time, it can be compounded on most days, in most hours.

Incense of Fumigation

Effective if used in a new house or dwelling before you actually take possession. If purchased, or rented, from another person, use *after* the old tenant has vacated if possible, if not, then use on the day of taking over the property. If the 'atmosphere' seems 'evil', use the 'Incense of Annihilation' plus an appropriate banishing ritual and/or delay your entrance date. You can burn an appropriate incense according to the day you enter the property and perhaps one of the following: Moon Incense for domestic felicity; Jupiter incense for money and 'luck' in general; Venus incense for harmony, happiness, social and congenial companionship; Saturn incense for stability of tenure or if the property is old. Remember these are 'aids' and you will not be handed any of the above just because you have burned a few grains of the appropriate incense, you have to play your part too. Incense of Fumigation consists of the following:

Camphor	Nutmeg
Myrtle	Aloeswood or
	Lign Aloes

Tuesday proves to be the best time for compounding this incense, in the hours of Mars or Pluto.

Khyphi Incense
The recipes for the famous Egyptian Khyphi Incense are numerous, each writer has his, or her, own personal choice of ingredients.

Incense 1	*Incense 2*	
Resin	Dragon's Blood	½ part
Galingal Root	Galingal Root	1 part
Mastic	Juniper Berries	1 part
Myrrh	Sweet Rush	1 part
Juniper Berries	Broom Flowers	1 part
Honey	Mastic	1 part
Wine	Myrrh	1 part

These two recipes do not contain the magical 'sixteen ingredients' as given by Plutarch (see section on 'Egypt'), but then neither does the recipe I use, based on the Eber's Papyrus.

Resin	Mastic
Galingal Root	Grapes
Juniper Berries	Honey
Root of Aromatic Rush	Wine
Asphaltus	Myrrh

General Incense

Musk	2 parts	Powdered Cinnamon	5 parts
Powdered Orris		Powdered Myrrh	5 parts
Root	3 parts	Powdered	
Patchouli Leaves	3 parts	Sandalwood	15 parts
Benzoin	3 parts	Frankincense	15 parts

Mix the above ingredients well together for an incense that can be burned at any time, mix at any convenient time.

Incense Cones

Powdered Charcoal		Powdered Benzoin	1 part
	6 parts	Potassium Nitrate	1 part
Powdered Myrrh	5 parts	Oil of	
Enough mucilage of		Sandalwood	2-3 drops
Tragacanth for binding		Oil of Bergamot	2-3 drops

Mix the powders well, add your oils, then add enough Tragacanth to give you a fairly stiff paste. Form into cones of convenient size and dry out in a warm place. Make sure they are dried out thoroughly.

N.B. When mixing your ingredients for incenses it is better to let the mixture stand overnight to 'take'. Be a little sparing with the oils until you gain experience, so that you do not make the mixture too soggy. Remember, it is easier to add a little more of the oils to the mixture, than to take away what is already there. If it is rather sticky, add more dry ingredients until the right texture is attained.

Sachet Bag

Powdered Orris		Patchouli Leaves	4 parts
Root	16 parts	Cloves	2 parts
Sandalwood	12 parts	Pimento	2 parts
Lavender Flowers	8 parts	Coriander Seeds	2 parts
Dried Rose Leaves	8 parts		

This is a very common recipe. Mix these ingredients well, then add the essence of any (or all) of the following: oil of lavender, musk, civet or ambergris. Mix so that no part of the preparation is soggy and then place into prepared, clean linen sachets.

Some Original Recipes

The following recipes were taken from a very old book loaned by a friend and dated 1824. However, some of the items are now very expensive and you may feel it extravagant to use them in the quantities recommended. If you feel you would like to try them, perhaps you could modify the formulas to suit your own needs.

To Make Aromatic Pastils

Beat and sift the following ingredients to make up 1 lb (450g) of mixture: coriander seed, gum benzoin, oil of rhodium, essence of lemon, essence of bergamotte, and oil of lavender. Add spirit of benjamin and 1 lb (450g) of gum benzoin. Dissolve some clear common gum arabic in a quantity of rose water, to give quite a thick consistency, and add sixty drops of musk.

Mix the whole together, so as to make a stiff paste, which may be made into small cones or balls. Dry them thoroughly before storing, otherwise they will become mouldy. These pastils are particularly useful in rooms where the sick or the dead have lain.

To Make Pastils for Perfuming Sick Rooms

Powder separately the following ingredients and then mix: 1 lb (450g) of gum benzoin, 8 oz. (225g) of gum storax, 1 lb (450g) of frankincense, and 2 lb (900g) of fine charcoal. Add to this composition the following liquids: 6 fl.oz. (175ml) of tincture of benzoin, 2 fl.oz. (50ml) of essence of ambergris, 1 fl.oz. (25ml) of essence of musk, 2 fl.oz. (50ml) of almond oil, and 4 fl.oz. (100ml) of clear syrup. Mix these into a stiff paste, form into conical pastils and dry in the sun. If more liquid should be required for the paste, add warm water.

To Make Perfumed Bags for Drawers and Clothes

Cut, slice and mix well together, in the form of very coarse powder, the following ingredients: 2 oz. (50g) of yellow sanders, 2 oz. (50g) of coriander seeds, 2 oz. (50g) of orris root, 2 oz. (50g) of calmus aromaticus, 2 oz. (50g) of cloves, 2 oz. (50g) of lavender flowers, and 1 lb (450g) of oak shavings. When properly mixed stuff into small linen bags, and place them in drawers, wardrobes, etc., which are either musty, or liable to become so.

APPENDIX

Table of Planetary Hours

After Sunrise	SUN.	MON.	TUES.	WED.	THURS.	FRI.	SAT.	From Midnight
1st	Sun	Moon	Mars	Mercury	Jupiter	Venus	Saturn	12-1 a.m.
2nd	Venus	Saturn	Sun	Moon	Mars	Mercury	Jupiter	1-2 a.m.
3rd	Mercury	Jupiter	Venus	Saturn	Sun	Moon	Mars	2-3 a.m.
4th	Moon	Mars	Mercury	Jupiter	Venus	Saturn	Sun	3-4 a.m.
5th	Saturn	Sun	Moon	Mars	Mercury	Jupiter	Venus	4-5 a.m.
6th	Jupiter	Venus	Saturn	Sun	Moon	Mars	Mercury	5-6 a.m.
7th	Mars	Mercury	Jupiter	Venus	Saturn	Sun	Moon	6-7 a.m.
8th	Sun	Moon	Mars	Mercury	Jupiter	Venus	Saturn	7-8 a.m.
9th	Venus	Saturn	Sun	Moon	Mars	Mercury	Jupiter	8-9 a.m.
10th	Mercury	Jupiter	Venus	Saturn	Sun	Moon	Mars	9-10 a.m.
11th	Moon	Mars	Mercury	Jupiter	Venus	Saturn	Sun	10-11 a.m.
12th	Saturn	Sun	Moon	Mars	Mercury	Jupiter	Venus	11-12 p.m.

Table of Planetary Hours (contd.)

After Sunrise	SUN.	MON.	TUES.	WED.	THURS.	FRI.	SAT.	From Noon
13th	Jupiter	Venus	Saturn	Sun	Moon	Mars	Mercury	12-1 p.m.
14th	Mars	Mercury	Jupiter	Venus	Saturn	Sun	Moon	1-2 p.m.
15th	Sun	Moon	Mars	Mercury	Jupiter	Venus	Saturn	2-3 p.m.
16th	Venus	Saturn	Sun	Moon	Mars	Mercury	Jupiter	3-4 p.m.
17th	Mercury	Jupiter	Venus	Saturn	Sun	Moon	Mars	4-5 p.m.
18th	Moon	Mars	Mercury	Jupiter	Venus	Saturn	Sun	5-6 p.m.
19th	Saturn	Sun	Moon	Mars	Mercury	Jupiter	Venus	6-7 p.m.
20th	Jupiter	Venus	Saturn	Sun	Moon	Mars	Mercury	7-8 p.m.
21st	Mars	Mercury	Jupiter	Venus	Saturn	Sun	Moon	8-9 p.m.
22nd	Sun	Moon	Mars	Mercury	Jupiter	Venus	Saturn	9-10 p.m.
23rd	Venus	Saturn	Sun	Moon	Mars	Mercury	Jupiter	10-11 p.m.
24th	Mercury	Jupiter	Venus	Saturn	Sun	Moon	Mars	11-12 a.m.

The Table consists across the top, of the seven days of the week. Below each day a list of the planets, one for each hour of the day. The right-hand side shows the hours as shown on a clock face. On the left-hand side headed 'After Sunrise' the consecutive twenty-four hours of the day. There are two methods of using this Table.

In the first system you look down the column of the day you are working in and find the planet you are working under, move along horizontally to the right-hand column, and the time will be shown on that day for that particular planet.

In the second system, the day is assumed only to have commenced at the actual time of sunrise, so you use the far-left column. You find the exact time of sunrise for the locality in which you are operating your ritual in hours and minutes; the first hour after that time is the first hour after sunrise, the second hour after sunrise is the next and so on. This system gives long days in summer and short in winter.

In the use of either system there is one precaution that must be observed. The Table is given in Greenwich Mean Time, so during British Summer Time (or any Daylight Saving Times elsewhere) one hour must be added to the Table. When B.S.T. is over and the hour removed, use the Table as given. Remember this or you will be working in the wrong hour during this period.

When the hours of the planets Uranus, Neptune and Pluto are required, use the hours of Saturn for Uranus, Jupiter for Neptune and Mars for Pluto; likewise with the days of the week, use Saturday for Uranus, Thursday for Neptune and Tuesday for Pluto.

INDEX